DON VESUVIO
The Story of Father Borrelli

DON VESUVIO

The Story of Father Borrelli

Mary Bodley

BACHMAN & TURNER
LONDON

First published 1974

© MARY BODLEY

ISBN 0 85974 006 4

Printed and bound by Butler & Tanner Ltd, Frome
and London, for the publishers, Bachman & Turner,
11 Smith Street, Chelsea, London SW3 4 EE

CONTENTS

Wherefore by their
fruits ye shall
know them
Matthew VII 20

My first book to my first
patron, my mother

CHAPTER 1

MARIO'S DREAM

CRASH! Bang! Wallop! Fountains of coffee shot up into the air, there was the noise of breaking china, an astonished twelve-year-old Neapolitan boy lay sprawling on the hard lava-cobbled pavement, his freshly laundered white jacket stained with coffee and milk.

He struggled painfully to his feet, carefully collected the broken cups and saucers and put them on the small metal tray whose paper tray-cloth, once so crisp and white, was now limp and soggy with the browny liquid floating all over the tray.

Ruefully he looked at the small square post-box which, as is usual in Italy, was fixed to the wall of a nearby house. He must have been day-dreaming to have bumped into it like that. Well, he didn't really want to run errands for the barber—kind though he might be. He didn't really want to sit in the barber's shop all day, ready to run out and get cups of coffee and anise, or refreshments of any kind, for the customers. It was not a very important job; it was not being anybody much; it was not even leading anywhere. Other boys went to school, for a start. . . other boys' parents had enough money to pay the fees! He reproved himself. There were other boys again who were far worse off than he was, in the Naples of 1934—had he not seen them himself? Homeless boys who ran about the streets, so poor that they had to beg for money and hang around the pavement cafés asking people to let them eat the crusts round their pizzas. He, at least, lived with his family and slept cosily tucked up in a warm bed at night with sheets, pillows and blankets. And the homeless boys? Where did *they* sleep, he wondered?

There he was, day-dreaming again! He pulled himself together, realising with an awful sinking feeling that he would have to own up to the barber about spilling the coffee and breaking the cups—and to his mother, too. The prospect seemed appalling. How could he say he was not looking where he was going, that he was not really doing his job properly, was not taking care of the tray at all? What would

11

his employer say? Would he give him the sack? For all his longing to leave his job, he knew he had to keep on because he had to earn his living. Yet he would never have thought of making up an excuse, for it was not in his nature to tell lies. An explanation and an apology had to be given. It was all a nightmare to a sensitive boy of twelve.

When he started to walk off he found that his feet just would not take him to the barber's shop. Instead, they walked him straight to his mother.

But if he thought that he would find more understanding from her than from the barber, he was mistaken!

"Mario! However did you get yourself in such a mess! Come here!" She got hold of him and gave him a good hiding. Poor Mario! The misery within him welled up and he howled.

"Give me that filthy jacket—here's tomorrow's laundered one. Put it on, blow your nose and go straight back to the shop with the tray, and tell them what happened."

Mario felt very sorry for himself as he entered the barber's shop, but, to his surprise, the incident was forgiven and quickly forgotten.

It often happens, however, that when people are really upset in some way, they suddenly see what really matters about themselves, their lives. It is as if they weigh the misery of what has happened to them against some other misery to find out which is heavier. This is what happened to Mario. He found that the misery he felt at being

12

spanked and at being so silly as to fall over was not half the weight of the misery he felt at keeping the secret of what he wanted to be when he grew up.

He sat down as usual, waiting for orders, and soon forgot all about the morning's mishaps, realising that there were far more important things in the world to worry about. He thought of himself as a grown man. He wanted to be somebody whom people would look up to, not a nonentity; he wanted above all, to help people.

Suddenly he felt that someone was looking at him. Looking up, he saw that his great hero, a priest called Don Nobilione, was smiling at him in the mirror. Their eyes met, and without saying a word it was as if they had a conversation. "Never mind about this morning, Mario, you're a good boy and we two are good friends, aren't we?" "Yes, we are, I knew you'd understand."

Soon, Don Nobilione got up to leave. Mario took the flat clerical hat down from the peg and dusted it carefully with the palm of his hand . . . life had begun to go on again and life was full of hope once more.

Suddenly, without even thinking about it, he knew he could always say anything to Don Nobilione; he knew the priest would never laugh at him or be too cross with him. If he ever did something wrong, he knew Don Nobilione would be stern but loving, and he would never laugh at even his wildest dreams. Even his secret misery, which he had just discovered was the greatest weight he had to bear and which he had kept in his heart for so long. In his love for Don Nobilione, he found that he was actually saying his dream out loud.

"Father . . . I . . . I want to be a priest."

"Then you will have to go to school," answered Don Nobilione.

In these two small sentences all his life seemed to have changed. Don Nobilione seemed to accept his dream without question; this meant that Mario was no longer the barber's boy whose secret was that he hoped one day to be a priest, but a boy who had quite definitely decided to be one and who would go to school to prepare himself for this.

When people are fond of music—as Mario was, of course, because all Neapolitans are fond of music—they often find themselves remembering sad tunes on occasions when they themselves are sad, jolly tunes when they are feeling full of fun, and noble, inspiring music when something very marvellous happens to them. At that moment Mario began remembering the grandest and most inspiring music he had ever heard.

The music came to an abrupt stop, however, as he heard Don
Nobilione ask: "And what does your mother say about it?"

Mario had just not had the courage to tell his mother at all. For
one thing, he knew that his parents could hardly afford the school fees.

Don Nobilione seemed to know what he was thinking! He put his
hand on Mario's shoulder and said quietly: "Shall we tell her
together?"

"When? Tonight?" It had to be at once. Mario could not have
endured it any longer.

"Very well, my son, tonight." Don Nobilione gave him one of his
kindly smiles.

Mario took great care to tell him how to get to his house, and said
goodbye.

Oh! He could hardly keep still—so happy was he!

*   *   *

When he had finished work and walked home as usual, he saw
everything as if he were seeing it for the first time.

The people living in single ground-floor rooms opening with wide
doors on to the pavement, in the crowded maze of streets in the
poorer quarters, were as usual standing in their doorways and chatting to each other after their day's work, their children playing on
the pavement. Inside, some rooms showed a domestic scene as the
mother put a large bowl of pasta on the table while the family came
in to eat. Some rooms were dark but some had a bright light shining
where old and young women sat around the table sewing busily, for
they earned their living by dressmaking and worked till late hours.

Down some dark alleys as Mario passed he could see those poorest
of boys, the "Scugnizzi", dressed in torn and dirty clothes, darting
across and picking up apple peelings which someone had thrown
into the road, or some other waste food, and eating it, or gazing
hungrily at the windows of small food shops and bakeries. He felt
very sorry for them, because they had no fathers or mothers to look
after them. Some of his own elation vanished.

But he was seeing everything as if for the first time—and, seeing
all this, he knew that one day he would have the chance of helping
them in their suffering.

*   *   *

Mario waited for Don Nobilione at the foot of the big stone staircase in the cool entrance to the flats where his family lived. He loved

14

this large stone-floored entrance; its arch on the roadway was made of massive blocks of beautifully-hewn stone, and the walls inside were of coral-coloured plaster. Now that it was evening, the place was cooler than ever, and he was pleased that this was so, as the day had been so very hot and tiring.

Before Mario had time to ponder much on the things that were happening to him, Don Nobilione swept in through the archway, his black soutane swishing. "Well, my son, shall we go up?"

Mario's mother *was* surprised. She had always thought of her son as a rather naughty little boy who used to have an awful temper when he was smaller, who used to throw stones up at fruit-trees in the park so as to bring down some fruit to eat, who used to run out into the road and cling on to the backs of passing trams.

She knew he would grow out of it in time; she had always said to herself "Boys will be boys." And it was true. This side of his nature seemed to be improving lately. But . . . there was this morning's incident of the spilt coffee—really, a boy of his age should not go rushing about like that!

Now here he was in front of her—could she believe her ears?—saying he wanted to be a . . . priest! And, what was even more strange, Don Nobilione, in his kindness, was actually backing him up! She could not understand it!

"But . . . *Mario* . . . a priest!" She waved her hands in the air, incapable of finding words to express her feelings.

15

The money . . . where would the money come from for his schooling? "We are only poor craftsmen-jewellers. How could we possibly find the money! No, Don Nobilione, it is really extremely kind of you to take an interest in my son like this, but Mario can never be a priest."

Mario's legs felt suddenly heavy, and a lump came into his throat, but he manfully managed to control himself. A grey gloom seemed to settle on everything. Time stood still.

He roused himself. What was that Don Nobilione was saying?

He was looking straight at Mario with a wonderful look on his face which meant that he had complete confidence in him; and the words he was saying were these:

"*I* will pay. Don't worry, I will pay for everything—Mario's school fees, his books, anything he needs. I will myself apply for him to enter the Apostolic School for Boys."

That night, when he said his prayers—as he *nearly* always did—he said "Thank you" to God for all the wonderful things that had happened to him. Things he would never have believed could have happened when he had said his prayers that morning.

CHAPTER 2

FOUR YEARS OF POVERTY

NAPLES is renowned for the beauty of the bay, for the blueness of the sea, for Capri, an island just off the mainland, for Vesuvius, and for a long promenade with expensive hotels. Then there is the old port, where Nelson anchored his ship on a visit to the ambassador.

There are many beautiful and historic houses, churches, and other buildings. Pompeii is nearby, and the museums are full of a heritage

of art, yet there are vast areas in Naples which are nothing more than slums; there the people are very poor indeed, and for some, nearly all of them, there is no possibility of gettting richer because there are just not any jobs to be had.

Some people are lucky enough to be in a family which has done the same work for generations, and, even if the work brings in just a bare living and no chance of better living conditions, they thank God that they have work to do and carry on doing it in the best way they can.

Mario's parents were people like this. His father's family had been craftsmen-jewellers for generations, mending jewellery. It seems strange that with all this poverty Neapolitans have any jewellery to mend, but Naples is a strange place: there are many poor but also many very rich people, and the very rich people don't want to have anything to do with the poor; they rather despise them, and think it beneath their dignity even to remember that they exist. Yet exist they do, and when one of the richer ladies loses a stone from her ring (one of those large, ornate rings the rich Neapolitans love to wear) she takes it to a fashionable jeweller, who sends it for repair to the quarter of the workers in precious metals. Here, in much the same way as in medieval times, lives a whole community of people whose livelihood depends on the making and mending of jewellery. Here live and work craftsmen who can design and make brooches, earrings, bracelets, or any other article of jewellery, those who delicately repair broken jewellery, those who gild in silver or gold.

Yes, they live and work here; and work really does mean work in Naples, for a lot of it has to be done in order to earn a very little money. Everywhere in Naples, late at night, people can be seen working. From buses and trams, as one journeys along at eight or nine o'clock, one can see the light burning in many a room full of women, sitting around a table dressmaking, not for themselves but to sell. Makers of chairs, seat menders, and other people who have their own businesses, can also be seen. The workers in precious metals are no exception.

Mario's father's trade was silver gilding, and his assistants were one of Mario's brothers, his sisters, and his aunts; while another of Mario's brothers was a jeweller. Between his various jobs at different barbers, Mario had helped his father too, but he had always known that this work was not for him.

Mario now went to school! He became quite a different boy. Gone were his childish tantrums and little naughtinesses. Gone too was his day-dreaming—he had no need for that now.

When he passed the barber's shop on his way to school, with the books under his arm which Don Nobilione had bought for him, he often peeped in to see if he were there and to wave a friendly and loving "Good morning, Father!"

To be at school! To have this chance of learning, of becoming a well-educated person able to hold his own with other well-educated

people when he grew up, was a wonderful thing to be happening to *him*. But he knew he had a lot of leeway to make up if he were to catch up with the boys who had been at school since they were five or six. He knew also that he had to show his teachers that he wanted to learn, and he had to show Don Nobilione that he was making good progress, or else the good priest would not feel like giving up so much of his meagre supply of money for his schooling.

Mario felt that there was within him, part of his very character, a strong sense of discipline, of endurance, and it was this side of his character which he brought into play at that time.

He disciplined himself to study hard, to give up every spare minute he had after school to reading and re-reading his school-books, going over the lessons again and again until he knew everything perfectly. He forced his brain to work promptly, to grasp ideas quickly; very soon he didn't even have to go over the lessons again, as he had understood them the first time.

The first year at school he showed good progress, and the teachers saw that this boy was really determined to achieve success. His mother was very pleased, and Don Nobilione very proud; he had never had any doubts about Mario's ability to succeed, and now he was confirmed in his high opinion of him.

A great shock was to come to Mario, however. Don Nobilione

had not realised that educating a boy would be so costly, and he just could not keep on paying, for he was very poor and had been spending more money than he could afford.

Mario's mother heroically stepped into the breach. Rather than Mario having to stop going to school, she decided that she herself would go out to work and earn the money needed to keep him there.

Well, of course, there was nothing for it but that he simply had to become top of his class—and stay there. His mother would never have continued to give out her hard-earned money if he had been one of those boys who do not take an interest in their lessons, who say they hate going to school, or play truant.

How difficult it was for Mario's mother! She had the flat to look after as usual, all the washing and ironing to do, all the cooking and shopping for her family of five and her husband, and then, on top of all that she went out to work all day. It was so hard for her. She was always tired at night when Mario sat at the kitchen-table doing his homework while she stitched and patched the clothes of all the family to make them last.

At the end of the week, when she counted what money she had left to give to Mario to buy exercise books, there was never enough.

There was never enough money, there were never enough books! Mario had to borrow them from his friends—there was no library anywhere—and, of course, his friends wanted them back again as quickly as possible. It was then that Mario invented for himself a new training idea: he made himself read the passages he needed in the text-books, and memorise them, and he became so adept at this that he could soon learn things with great speed. This was very good for him as it made his brain work quickly, so that he could learn more and more.

All of these four years were very hard ones for him. He studied incessantly, without having any fun at all—no cinema, no holidays, no trips; only work, work, work, and all around him poverty. His clothes became more and more worn. As for his shoes—whenever they got holes in the soles there was not enough money to send them to be mended, so Mario used to go into his father's workshop, cut a length of brass wire, and coil it up in the hole.

These four years were 1936, 1937, 1938 and 1939. There was unemployment and poverty in England too during that time, but in Naples it was far worse.

Poverty in Naples means, even now, being able to eat meat only just once a week because the prices are too high, not being able to eat much fruit either, or vegetables, for the same reason, but living mainly on various kinds of pasta.

Poverty in Naples means not being able to buy enough fuel to keep warm with in the cold winter months, and having to rely on charcoal burnt in an old-fashioned stove, or bits of odd wood and broken boxes picked up in the street.

Poverty in Naples means living in one or two rooms in dark, damp, uncomfortable old-fashioned houses, their outside walls covered

with coloured plaster which is always falling off because no one has enough money to replace it. It means having to wash in cold water in a basin on the kitchen table.

Poverty in Naples means never having a bedroom to yourself but having to share the same room, and often the same bed, with your brothers and sisters.

Yet the Neapolitan endures all this and remains very cheerful, very friendly, very kind. He sings in the streets and while working. And the sheets, which are hung out on lines jutting out over the road, having been washed in nothing but ice-cold water, are dazzlingly white.

CHAPTER 3

THE SEMINARY

THE Rector of the Capodimonte seminary was a very learned man and a very good one, and he was also very thin and *very* tall!

One day, as he sat at his desk in his oak-panelled study busily labouring through the mounds of work he had to do for the seminary, he was told that a Monsignore from Rome, whom he had never met before, had come to see him. The good Rector was glad to put aside his work for a while and, relaxed, awaited his visitor.

The door opened. "Ah, Monsignore, I am glad to make your acquaintance. Your Reverence. . ."

The Rector was astonished at the appearance of this guest, but good breeding compelled him to say nothing and appear as charmingly polite as he could. "Have you travelled comfortably, Monsignore?" he said, while secretly marvelling that there could be someone so much taller than his own six feet—for this visitor was so tall that it was almost unbelievable. Yes, he mused, almost unbeliev . . .

Then, before his very eyes, the Monsignore disintegrated—the top half of him seemed to crumble up, while on the floor his lower half seemed to be writhing with a will all its own.

The Rector was alarmed—perhaps the Monsignore was having a fit. His good nature asserted itself and he rushed forward and bent over the prostrate figure. "My dear friend—what has happened?"

Words did not seem to be able to come from the mouth of the figure lying on the floor, but somehow the face, bereft of clerical hat, seemed familiar. Two mischievous greeny-blue eyes looked up pleadingly and guiltily at the Rector.

"Please, it was a joke: Giovanni acted the legs part and I acted the top part—it was a joke . . . well, it's Carnival time after all, and you see . . ." The Rector cut this explanation short.

"Mario Borrelli, get yourself tidied up and then come back here with Giovanni—but both on your own two feet," he added with a twinkle in his eye.

So now you know that Mario passed his entrance exam to the seminary—in fact he passed with top marks. But, as you see, he was still very high-spirited and his studies were enlivened by the most amazing scrapes into which he got himself—and others.

The class in which he was had twenty boys, and as they got up to all sorts of pranks together—as a bunch—they were nicknamed "the Bunch of Grapes".

One evening in the dormitory, just as they were climbing into bed, shrill screams were heard from one of the boys, followed by one voice and then another shouting: "The Pope! The Pope! The Pope is being eaten by crocodiles!"

Mario, looking innocent, lay in his bed pretending to be asleep.

Each term, the seminarists elected one of their number as Pope and others as Cardinals, and so on, and this term it was a member of the Bunch of Grapes who was "Pope".

Of course, the boys always teased and ragged their Pope and his Cardinals, and so it was that Mario had collected as many lizards as he could on the hot, sunny terrace and had put them in the bed of the Pope.

The seminary is not at all the dull place which some people might imagine it would be! The young men there are hardly more than boys, and just as full of high spirits as their brothers of the same age all over the world who are studying for other careers.

Seminary, by the way, means, from Latin, a place where the good seed is sown. The good seed being new priests to go out and do good in the world.

Mario had a marvellous time. He continued studying Greek and Latin, which he had already started at the Apostolic School, and now he started learning English, Spanish and German. He also took part in games, which he loved, and became very good at football. But, of course, the main study was how to become a good priest, so as to help people with their problems, and pray to God to make him worthy of his calling.

While Mario was in the seminary, the war was on, and Hitler's German troops were stationed in an Italy ruled over by the dictator Mussolini; these two were the enemies of Britain, France, America, and their allies in Europe.

One of the big schemes to end the war was to land a British force in Sicily to fight through Italy, and so end the domination of Italy by Mussolini and force Hitler's troops out. Sicily was invaded in July 1943, and Italy surrendered on September 7, but the Germans still occupied the mainland. This meant the Allies bombing enemy-held territory immediately behind the lines, and so it was that for the first time in his life Mario saw war and was in a town under bombing.

The seminary was situated high above Naples itself, at a place called Capo di Monte, which means, really, "Mountain-top". Night after night Mario stood transfixed at the long windows of the seminary which had lost all their glass as a result of a bomb-blast—just as had happened in England when the Germans were bombing there.

He stood transfixed; he was terrified at seeing so many of the buildings he knew crumbling and going up in flames and exploding from the bombs, and yet he could not tear himself away. He had discovered that one can reduce fear by eating, so, as he stood there, he chewed

crusts of old dry bread, shrivelled-up chestnuts, or other things of that sort.

But it didn't help much when the German tanks turned their guns on the seminary!

Naples became almost a besieged city, with fighting in the streets. There was no water, and food was getting short. The British and American troops were simply marching towards Naples unopposed, as many of the Italians in the surrounding countryside, happy that the Allies had come to turn out the Germans, joined in the fighting themselves.

In Naples, the people fought to turn out the Germans, and there was a battle lasting four days which was called "the Four Days of Naples" while the British were on the way in to back them up. The people who helped more than anyone else were the little Scugnizzi boys, the boys with no homes, no mothers and fathers to love them— the boys who were so despised by the people of Naples that no one bothered to give them food or shelter. They were the ones who had the great heart and the great love to fight for their native city, some even giving their lives.

Naples is built on ground which slopes up from the sea. The poorer quarters are down by the harbour and the station at the bottom of the

slope, but if you take a bus to the top of the slope you find yourself passing through more and more beautiful suburbs, terraces over the sea, lots of trees and a few gardens.

To go from the suburbs at the top of the slope to the main town at the foot of it you need not take a bus, but the "Funicular" which is a lift, attached, as it were, at one side to the sloping hillside.

This lift was the scene of much activity during the Four Days of Naples. The Scugnizzi knew it, and the various tunnels and passages which are always part of railways, as well as they knew the backs of their hands, because they always lived out in the open.

They themselves held the position of the lift terminus, and defended it against the Germans.

On October 1, the British and Americans arrived, and the German occupation was over.

CHAPTER 4

MATERDEI

THE war in Europe was to last for nearly another two years, and Mario's life in the seminary for another two years after that. In 1947, when he was twenty five years old, he was ordained, and became . . . Father Mario Borrelli.

How wonderful it was to be alive, to be young, and, above all, to have dedicated his life to the service of God! He felt he was just as much a Disciple of Jesus Christ as any of the Disciples who were actually alive when He was, and he prayed in this great upsurge of joy that Christ would guide him to know what was the best use he could make of his life.

He felt that his life, the very fact that he was alive, was a gift from God, and he wanted to use this precious gift to the full. What was there that he alone could do? Was there some special work which Christ knew needed doing in the world and which could be done by Mario, and Mario alone? Or was he more useful doing the day-to-day routine of parish work? How Father Mario prayed in those days!

His very soul burned within him, so keen was he on doing just what Jesus Christ wanted him to do. All sorts of things presented themselves! "Which one, oh, which one," he thought, "is the right thing for me?"

There was his teaching job at a Catholic school for boys, there was the parish of S. Gennaro a Materdei, to which he was attached, his early morning masses for factory workers, his Youth Club work, his work among the poor children, and his home-made puppet-shows of religious themes made specially light and amusing for very young children.

He lived at home with his mother, and was happy to be able to keep her company.

The Youth Club interested him very much indeed. These clubs had been kept going all through the Mussolini regime by the Church, and now that the war was over they were needed even more, to help

young people to cope with the bewilderingly new post-war life. Father
Mario felt that this was a way in which he really could give of his
best; he was young himself and his teenage days were near enough
for him to remember what they had been like, so he knew he was
well-fitted to help young people.

In his parish there was a tumbledown baroque church, dedicated
to Mary Mother of God, *Materdei*. It had not been used as a church

for a long time—in fact since before the war—and bombing had
added to its dereliction. This church he was given to use as a Youth
Club.

Young Father Mario walked to the Materdei one evening after
his work at the school; up the steep ramp which led from the main
road, past the little sanctuary to the Madonna, a statue of Our Lady
placed in a niche above a little chapel. It seemed to him that the
poverty-stricken world about him was blessed and hallowed by this
shrine, and he crossed himself as he passed.

Up, up, and up a steeper ramp he trudged; there was a tall wall
on one side of the ramp and it was damp and black and dirty. Little
children dressed in torn, dirty clothes were playing beside it. The
pavement, which was also black because it was made with stones
hewn from the lava of Vesuvius, had not been swept for many days
and was strewn with all kinds of refuse. Empty cigarette-boxes, bits
of straw and rags, sweepings from the nearby houses, fruit-peel and

all sorts of other things. Across the ramp on the opposite side to the wall was a row of mean houses, the ground floors of which consisted of a single, large, dark room, which had a single door opening out onto the pavement—the houses he had known since childhood. These doors were open, as it was a warm evening, and some of the children playing by the wall were called in by harsh-voiced mothers as they heard the steps of the stranger approach. Some had sullen faces, some had hopeless apathetic faces, some had wary faces, all summing him up, looking at him. Father Mario glanced at them and said: "*Buona sera*—good evening." But they only grunted in reply. They

seemed to be saying to themselves: "Oh! Here's a priest. Priests are supposed to help people, but we, the poor, the oppressed, no one ever helps us, anyone can see that, because otherwise we would not be in this plight."

As Father Mario crested the brow of the rise, he turned left slightly to go on his way, but his attention was drawn to a large clearing in front of him. Here some houses had received a direct hit during the bombing, and the rubble of the broken homes lay all about. In addition to this, the local people had used it as a refuse dump, throwing all sorts of things they did not want there: old cars, bicycle wheels, broken packing cases, cardboard boxes, rags, old shoes. Right in front of all this, spilling out onto the road, was a huge pile of ordinary rubbish which should have been in dustbins.

Father Mario knew that at the school, as in the wealthier residential areas, rubbish was collected every day in the earlier hours of the morning; but he also knew that here, as in every poor quarter, the rubbish was not collected till much later in the day or even not at all; or perhaps, as a special condescending favour, once a week. He also knew that the poor people were far too poor to buy themselves dustbins and that they therefore threw their rubbish on piles such as this, out on the road. And he also knew, of course, that illness and serious disease could be the only outcome of this practice. The stinking piles of refuse, rotting in the hot sun, day after day, were accepted as part of the everyday scene.

He continued on his way, and the actual way itself, the very road which he had to tread, was no rougher than the spiritual road he had chosen to follow: the road was no more than a track, uneven and dirty, made of old stones and brickbats. He turned a sharp corner and was nearly knocked over by a young boy tearing round it on a bicycle!

His sharp eyes detected something which looked like an animal darting about in the refuse heap, farther back, where the old junk was; it was not an animal, it was a small boy. A boy, not more than— who could tell his age? His eyes had the look of a hunted creature, his hair was matted with dirt, he was dressed in a pair of long trousers many sizes too big for him, a torn, filthy jacket and a pair of tennis shoes with holes in the caps, his toes poking through. Soon it became apparent to Father Mario that this creature was searching for what edible morsel he could find amongst the refuse. He was avidly searching there, his eyes gleaming whenever he saw something that might do, his bony claw-like hands snatching at the thing which he then conveyed to his mouth. A few feet away from him a dog, so thin that his ribs were showing, was also scavenging for food.

Father Mario's priest's heart was heavy with the misery of it all.

Suddenly he was in the little square where his bombed church was. It could hardly be called a Square, and in fact it was not called a *Piazza*, the Italian word for Square, but *Largo*, which means just a larger space than usual, for it was no more than a clearing in the vast maze of streets which opened up from every side.

The cobbles, still of lava-stone, were placed in a circular pattern with its centre in the middle of the Largo. Gaunt, dirty buildings ranged on either side. Some had cavernous archways like the one Father Mario had loved in his own house as a boy. Some had the washing still hanging out to dry in the last rays of the evening sun.

30

On one side was a mean café and on another some more tenement dwellings with the usual ground-floor room and doorway opening onto the road. Suspicious eyes followed him as he walked in, straight through the doorway by the side of the little tumbledown church.

"Father! You've come at last! We're all ready to begin. What shall we do first?" A group of happy, eager boys awaited him.

He felt heartened to think that he could help the younger generation, at least, to rise out of all the misery and squalor which surrounded them, and his spirits rose.

"We must get to work. Get the place clean for a start. I've got some tins of whitewash in the office, and some brushes; we'll get the work finished in no time." So saying, he swiftly undid the long row of buttons on his soutane and hung it up on a peg. He was dressed ready for work. A pair of dark trousers, one of the brilliant white shirts which his mother laundered for him with just as much loving care as she had lavished on his barber's boy's jackets all those years ago.

Father Mario was a swift worker, and soon was covering much more wall than the young boys. He chatted with them as he worked and laughed, and even sang with them the old Neapolitan songs they all knew and loved so well.

Two of the boys paused a while in their work to look at him. All the boys, it was true, were beginning to hero-worship him. "Look at Father Mario," one whispered to the other, "He doesn't even look like a priest, does he?" "No," said the other, "He just looks like . . . well . . . one of us!" And that, from the sons of the sullen tenement-dwellers, was a compliment indeed!

Well, thought Father Mario, his shirt-sleeves rolled up and his face splashed with distemper, that was one way in which he could, with his particular gifts, contribute something to the world in which he lived. He had a great affection for children, he was a born teacher at heart, and these two things combined gave him the particular talent of teaching young people, his personal religious character adding to this. To his mind, at the time, teaching young people to grow up into fine men and women, who could take their place in rebuilding the world shattered by war, seemed a very worthwhile job. Still, however, he felt, deep down within him, that this was not the thing which could become his life's work.

He felt so full of youthful vigour that he wanted to fill every hour of his day—and his day started very early in the morning with the first Mass.

He chose to say this Mass, not in the parish church where people came only if they could find the time to get there before the day's work but at the gates of a factory, so that the men and women working there had the chance to attend just before starting their shift.

* * *

Very early in the morning, when the streets of the poorer quarters of Naples were cool and fairly empty, long before any amount of traffic tumbled down the winding alleys or roared along the main roads, when the sky was pale gold and Vesuvius barely visible in the mist surrounding the bay, when the early-morning fishermen were out in their small, still boats, and only the most diligent housewives were sweeping the patch of pavement in front of their tenements, an old, grey, bulky car was to be seen rocking its way along the cobbled streets.

At the back of the car something was carefully packed and covered with a white cloth.

The driver was a very young priest who smiled and whistled as he drove along; his name—Father Mario Borrelli.

He drove on until he got to the outskirts of the city, where a large factory occupied a vast area of ground. At the gates, he stopped, but did not go in. He carefully took out the things from the back of the car and set up an altar.

Everything needed to say Mass was there—crucifix, chalice, cloths, vestments.

Very soon some of the factory workers began to arrive and he greeted them cheerfully. "*Come va*, Antonio—how are things?" "*Non c'e male*, not bad," answered Antonio. "And how are you getting on with your new job, Giuseppina?" "How are the children?" He chatted and joked with them easily, obviously enjoying it, and not being patronising one little bit. Soon quite a cluster of people were all round him, enjoying the company of this affable young man. "*Molto simpatico*," they whispered to each other, "A very agreeable person."

Suddenly, Father Mario's jovial mood changed. He was silent, and in a quiet voice he said: "Shall we begin the Mass now, my friends?" He was profoundly serious, transported into his sacramental and mystical life as he said the Mass, gave each one Communion and, finally, gave the Blessing.

Mass over, they cheerfully went in to work, but Father Mario was not alone. While the Mass had been on, a whole crowd of children had quietly crept up to see this strange sight—a church in the street.

Father Mario was in his element! He smiled broadly at them, patted the heads of the younger ones and spoke to the older ones as they beamed up at him with shining eyes. And then it was that another idea began to germinate in his fertile mind.

A few weeks later there was another package in the back of the car. When Father Mario set up his altar he left the other package where it was. The children were more than curious, they tiptoed round the car looking in even while the Mass was still going on. And when it was finished they waited with mounting excitement while Father Mario put the altar things back in and covered them up tenderly.

"Cosa c'e li dentro, Padre? Father, what is in there?" asked a tiny four-year-old.

"You wait and see!" answered Father Mario kindly, "You wait and see!"

The children edged closer and closer, so that when he had gathered the parcel in his arms, ready to take it out, he just couldn't move as they were all round him.

"Please give me a bit of space!" he said.

One of the older boys pulled some of the smaller children away. "Come away, you sillies, can't you see that Father can't move?!"

"Thank you! Thank you!" laughed Father Mario, but still the children practically clung to his soutane! This did not anger him, but rather pleased him. "How loving and trusting little children are," he thought. They had none of the suspicions of their elders, but how long would they be able to keep up this innocence? Soon they would come up against all the wickedness and trials of the world around them, people would deride them for trying to be good, would take advantage of their trusting natures and tell them to do things that were bad. The children, thinking that all grown-ups were to be obeyed, would obey, and do the wrong things which evil people would tell them to do. He had seen this happen often, especially in the shanty-town where lived people who were sometimes very bad— thieves, black-marketeers, murderers. These people thought nothing of teaching little boys to steal as soon as they could walk. Thought nothing of making little girls of six or seven fetch water in heavy buckets from the communal taps out in the streets near the shacks. Thought nothing of forcing both boys and girls to beg for money in the streets, making them look much poorer than they really were in order to attract pity. The children were cruelly treated and beaten if they did not do these things. *If anyone harm any of these little ones, it were better that a millstone were hung around his neck.* ... It was clear that Christ wanted people to teach children about Him; what a responsibility everyone had, thought Father Mario, and for a priest the responsibility was even greater; it amounted to an order which he had to honour. It was for this reason that he had brought along the mysterious parcel.

As he set the heavy parcel on the pavement, he unwrapped it and started to stand something up. The something looked like a huge rectangular box, a little higher than Father Mario himself; about three feet from the top there was a shelf. In front of the lower half hung a gaily-striped curtain, and the top, above the shelf, was painted like the decor of a stage. Curtains, like theatre curtains, hung in front at the top, like a pelmet, and there were two more ready to pull across from the sides. Father Mario closed them and went behind.

"*Un teatro!* A theatre!" exclaimed the children.

He stooped down and opened a large box. The children, of course, were round there with him; they crouched on the ground beside him and peered into the box. "*Bamboline!*" said the four-year-old in wonder, "Dollies!" and gazed incredulously at Father. Surely he was old enough to have stopped playing with dolls?

"*Sono le Sue, Padre?* Are they yours, Father?"

Father Mario turned an open, smiling face on the child: "Yes, little one, they are!"

"*Vedi!*" the little boy said triumphantly to his elder brother, who had been telling him not to be so silly as to think that Father still played with toys!

They were not dolls, however, but puppets. Mr. Punch and Mrs. Judy and other characters.

Father Mario placed the strings in the appropriate sockets and adjusted the puppets. He had been learning all this from the friend who had made the puppets and theatre-box for him. "Now all of you, away from here, go round to the front and . . . Our Performance Will . . ." and he opened the curtains "Begin!"

How the children gasped! Their own Punch and Judy show!

As a matter of fact, Punch and Judy shows are a traditional Neapolitan entertainment, Punch being called Pulcinella. This time, however, the scenes acted out by Punch and Judy and the others were not the usual traditional ones, for Father Mario had written the dialogue himself!

In the scenes he was teaching the children the simple rules of a good and happy life. To be always honest. To say their prayers night and morning, and always to live through every day with the

34

thought "God sees me—am I doing what is right and what he wants me to do?" uppermost in their minds.

The children loved the show, and they loved their Father Mario, and he himself felt that he had reached another milestone on his journey towards finding out what God really wanted him to do.

Still, he knew this was not the final answer; he was learning about himself, what his natural talents were, how he could get across to

people, what sort of people he was best at helping. All the things he had done were a sort of preparation for something else, but he did not know what that something else was.

He also did some work at about this time with his friend Ciccio, another young priest who had been in the seminary with him. The work was with a children's organisation which the Church had started, but after a time they both discovered that this particular field of work was not "them" and they stopped doing it.

*   *   *

Then another interesting thing happened to him, which was even another form of preparation for what he eventually came to know was his life's work. It happened like this.

Father Mario's holiday was spent taking part in a camp for young priests in the mountains. Being all young and in high spirits, they were keen on getting as much climbing as they possibly could, and they dressed not as priests but just as any other young man would for climbing. Because of his layman's clothes Father Mario could go into the neighbouring town and into the shops and cafés on the same level as anyone else. This meant more to him than he could have imagined because up to this time he had been so busy with his work that he had not taken much notice of the fact that most people were shy or antagonistic towards priests; but that they were so there was no denying. When a priest was talking to them they were specially respectful, talking only about agreeable things, never voicing any opinions against the Church; but they were often being insincere, because when the priest was not there they said just the opposite! Now that he was dressed like any young man, people talked to him in a very different way. They opened up their hearts to him in a way that no casual acquaintance had ever done before. This was a new world to Father Mario and he decided to profit by it.

Of course, although he looked different, he was still the same person, still wanting to help people more than ever. So he appeared to those he met as an extraordinarily nice young man, unselfish and kind, and everyone was his friend.

He had almost never had this freedom to mix with people before, and he felt that a priest's life was far too cut off from the lives of the very people he had to help spiritually. So he now went out of his way to know what people were really like. He wanted to know all about the problems and trials and worries that people had to face.

On certain days some strange-looking persons came into the town; they came on horses and went to the shops to buy provisions; they looked very secretive and very rough and uncouth, and, to cap everything, their skin was almost black with a deep ingrained kind of dirt. The shop people didn't really want to see them though they had to serve them, the townspeople stared unkindly at them, and the children giggled.

Father Mario was absolutely fascinated! He wanted to find out about people—well, here were some the like of whom he had never known existed. He would find out about them! He asked the local people who these others were, and got the answer that they were charcoal burners from the nearby hills.

After that there was no stopping him. He swiftly made friends with one or two of them and so surprised were they that anyone had talked to them at all that they actually talked and laughed with him. The townspeople thought him quite mad; they would never demean themselves by talking to such riff-raff; *they* were respectable citizens!

Seeing them so despised by the others made Father Mario feel a surge of compassion towards them. He was feeling the strength of his desire to stand up for the "underdog".

The charcoal-burners invited him to visit them in their camp up the mountain where they carried on their trade. Here he spent many happy hours with them, and, as the camp was far up the mountain, they used to send one of their horses down to the village for him every day. The horse arrived of its own accord and Father Mario had only to mount it for it to carry him directly to the charcoal-burners' camp. How strange it seemed! But it was all in keeping with the character of these people themselves, for they were fonder of doing things than of talking about them, a trait not often found in people generally. They were sincere, honest, thoughtful and . . . silent!

Every day Father Mario would bring presents for them—mostly tinned food, which was scarce and costly—and sweets for the youngsters.

When Sunday came he realised he would have to tell them he was a priest, and he felt he had been dishonest in not telling them before. He invited them to his camp where he himself was saying Mass, and wondered whether they would come. They came. They were all dressed up in their Sunday best and as clean as could be. After the Mass they thanked him very much indeed, but seemed rather more quiet than usual, which meant that they hardly talked at all!

For several days the horse did not come for him and Father Mario became very worried indeed. He searched his conscience, and remembered he had been dishonest in not telling them straightaway that he was a priest. These upright, silent people, who thought so much, had surely been weighing up his character . . . and found it lacking.

Then, one day, the horse came down the mountain again and stood quietly for him as it had done before. So happy was Father Mario then that he sunk his head into the horse's mane and breathed a prayer of thanks. As the horse took him higher and higher up the mountains he looked about him and felt his own happiness mingle with the beauty of the scenery, till, as an artist whose senses are heightened and sharpened by a scene which attracts him, he became more and more exultant . . . adoring God in the beauty of His creation.

When he reached the camp there was a happy reunion. Actually, what had happened was that they had been so astonished at finding him to be a priest that they did not know what to do! Although still liking him and wanting to talk to him and enjoy his company as before, they had thought him "too grand" for them. After thinking things over, however, they had decided that he was just himself, whether priest or layman, and so they sent the horse down to the village for him again as before.

By now he had learnt this: that he could teach; that he liked children; and that he had a flair for making friends with people—especially if he were not dressed as a priest.

CHAPTER 5

THE SCUGNIZZI OF NAPLES

NOW the time has come to put in a few words about the Scugnizzi. They are boys who have left home because they come from what we in Britain call "broken homes"; this means a family which is just as much broken, in the spiritual sense, as the bombed-out houses, past which Father Mario walked when he went to Materdei, were in the actual sense.

In these families, many things could cause the break-up. Perhaps the father was an habitual drunkard, using all the money, or most of it, on himself, thus making it impossible for the mother to stay at home and look after the family because she herself had to go out to work to earn the money to keep herself and her children. This, of course, means that she has to leave the children, always ten or so in Neapolitan families, at home on their own. Another cause of a break-up in a home could be that the mother has had a serious illness and has been in hospital for a long time, the father then having the impossible task of going to work all day *and* looking after the family —for working hours are very long in Naples. Sometimes the break-up occurs when the children have lost one or other of their parents and the widow or widower just can't cope alone. These, and many other things, contribute to a break-up in the smooth running and harmony of the family; quarrels are an everyday occurrence; the children are maltreated or ignored, and often end up by losing interest in their family altogether.

Then, of course, there is the problem of school. There is still today an acute shortage of teachers in the South of Italy, and, at the time in which this story is set, immediately after the War, the shortage was even greater. There was also a need for more school buildings. Tuition could only be given to each child for about three hours a day—morning or afternoon, but not both. As the vast majority of children, all over the world, get out of going to school if at all possible, one can well imagine that the children from the broken homes do this much more than those from normal homes where there is stricter parental control.

The situation in Naples was so completely different from that elsewhere that it is almost impossible for anyone who has not been there to imagine it. There was no "Welfare State" there. No Health Service, such as we have, which enables people to go to the doctor and get free treatment for even the most trifling complaint. No free dental treatment. No National Insurance which gives help in the form of family allowances, grants, and old-age pensions. No Social Security to ensure that everyone has enough money to live on. No free education at the period in time with which this book deals. How lucky we are in Britain, and we take it all for granted!

Because of all this, it is imperative for a Neapolitan to get as good a job as he can, and keep it at all costs! Because of the state of the economy, however, and because Southern Italy has been, historically and traditionally, regarded not as a "development area" but as an area in the backwoods and not to be bothered about, jobs are few and poorly paid. So there is great poverty. There are also great riches. When a Neapolitan gets a better job and becomes well-off, he generally pretends that he has never been poor—and Neapolitans are great actors, every moment of the day! He shows this by despising the poor, saying they are beneath his plane of existence altogether and no part of his life, thoughts or duties. The poorer Neapolitans, therefore, have a very tough time of it indeed. As one must needs eat and have a roof of sorts over one's head and bring up one's family as best one can, it is little wonder that the very poorest people of all sometimes sink to crime. Begging, stealing, dishonesty of all sorts, cruelty to children, smuggling, selling stolen goods, all these things go on in full measure. It is all a "vicious circle", because what is needed is education, and this the poorer people do not have.

On top of the poverty and hopelessness, the families are generally large. Even the families which neglect their children love having new babies. Everyone adores babies in Naples and makes a lot of fuss over them.

In the broken homes, however, as soon as the boys become old enough to walk they toddle along by the side of their fathers and if, as will probably be the case, the father is engaged in crime, they quickly learn all about the begging and stealing and selling of stolen goods that goes on. It is easy from there for the father to teach them to do all these things for themselves. It is an everyday sight in Naples to see a child, boy or girl, dirty and very thin, dressed in the most pitifully old clothes, begging for money outside a restaurant, or just along the road. These children are usually not begging for themselves but have to take the money to their parents. Sometimes the children have to pretend to be ill, have a bad foot or something like that, so as to evoke the sympathy of the passer-by. If they do not do as they are told they are beaten, so of course they go on.

The little girls are taught housework at an early age, and in the shanty-town it is taken for granted that girls of seven will fetch the water in very heavy pails from the communal taps which, in the midst of the shacks, are the only water supply. They are also, in broken

homes in the poorer quarters, expected to fetch the shopping, sweep out the rooms, and so on. These children look very much more grown-up in their features than they really are; they are usually very thin and have a sort of deep sadness in their expressions. They do not develop healthy-growing bodies but grow very slowly, remaining thin and small for a long time, and sometimes their bodies stay stunted even when they are grown-up.

When the children begin to grow up—always, remember, the whole family living in a one-roomed shack in the shanty-town or in one or two rooms on the ground floor of a tenement—they rely more and more on the street outside their home for extra space, as their mothers do when they hang out the washing on lines outside the doors and windows. The poorer families live on ground level because the rents are cheaper.

If the parents have been maltreating the child very badly and he has just about "had enough of it" it is very easy for him to wander off into the maze of streets which surround his home, thinking he could have a much happier time just playing on the streets. He says to himself . . .

"It would be nice to live out here on my own, much nicer than at home in that one room, all squashed-up, having to go out and beg for money to give father, being beaten if I don't get enough, not having enough to eat when I do come back, late at night, and then not being able to sleep because I'm in the big family bed with everyone else."

The parents, when they see that this boy does not come back home, as likely as not do not worry at all, but say something like this . . .

"Thank goodness for that! He's gone! Now we can buy food for one person less and that will save us money." Or else . . .

"That wretched boy! He used to bring us in money which we had taught him to steal, picking the pockets of tourists. Wait till we catch him! How we'll beat him!"

So off the boy goes because, as Father Mario discovered, "there is no love in the home".

Once on the streets, however, he has to find some food. He can still beg and pick pockets as he has been taught, and this can bring in a bit of cash. He can also steal food, fruit from barrows and fish from the fish stalls, bread from bakers' shops and milk from people's doorsteps, and all sorts of things from people's cars which he can later sell.

Then, when night comes, he has to sleep. The hot day temperature has dropped and he has to wrap himself up in something; he has to think what this will be. He can cover himself with anything he finds lying around in the road—something for which people no longer have any use, such as paper left over from the day's trade of the street vendors of fruit and vegetables at their stalls in the market: most of them keep a pile of newspaper handy to wrap things up, and in the night breeze it just blows about all over the place. He finds this keeps him quite warm. He can also use bits of sacking in which the vegetables have arrived from the growers, but there is not much else.

In the morning, if he wants to have a wash (and he probably does at first, because sleeping on the pavement is anything but clean, though after some months he will prefer to be dirty) he can do so at a fountain or use some outside tap in the shanty-town.

Then another day has begun and he is feeling hungry. He must steal some food, or starve.

After a few days of this he realises it is hard going all alone. He is beginning to find out that he is not just having a happy time playing on the streets; but even then it's far better than being at home, a home such as his.

Soon, he meets others in the same predicament as he is; but there is a difference—he is alone, they are in gangs. He begins to want the idea of a "home" even if his was so wretched. He wants companionship. He joins a gang.

The gang have been watching him all the time, though hidden. They have been sizing him up. They know by now what he is like and how they can use him.

There is a gang-leader whose law is absolute, and each member of the gang has his particular job. All money stolen has to be shared,

also food and stolen things. It all begins to seem what he has run away from all over again. Perhaps you can't get away from it in Naples, he thinks. But now it is all on a lower level, now he is almost as much a criminal as any adult member of the underworld.

He doesn't understand what is happening to him but he can't back out now, he can't "tell" because the gang would punish him in their own cruel way.

He has become one of the Scugnizzi of Naples.

CHAPTER 6

DECISION

ONE evening, Father Mario was on the bus, going home from his work at the school. It was the rush-hour. There were so many people in the bus—there always are in Naples in the rush-hour! They were all jam-packed, standing up all the way down the gangway so that it was impossible to move one way or another.

Father Mario was dreaming again, just as he had done that time all those years ago when he had fallen over with the tray of coffee, but this time what he did was to get off at the wrong stop! Well, with all that confusion it could easily be done.

He was still dreaming away, turning over in his mind what his life's work was to be when, wrapped in thought, he got off and found himself on the pavement. Looking round, he realised that he did not really know where he was. His bewilderment was soon checked, however, by another surprise.

"Mario!"

"Ciccio!"

They had not seen each other for a long time.

"Well, what are you doing now?"

They spoke simultaneously. The figures of the two young priests formed an interesting sight for the queuers for quite a while as they talked on and on, oblivious of time and of the many buses which came and went.

Somehow, the strange situation, the suddenness of finding Ciccio, had given Father Mario a jolt just as forcible as the jolt, both spiritual and physical, he had received when he fell over with the tray. He told Ciccio all about the factory workers, the puppet-show, the Youth Club, and of his search and his prayers for the really right thing to do with his life.

Then he found himself saying . . .

"Oh Ciccio, the children! They need helping more than anyone else; everyone needs help, I know, but it's so much worse for the children—they have not had time to learn about Christianity, to go to school, to know that there are good and evil people in the world before they are hurled into life. While they are still babies, almost, they have to face the hard realities of life, just as their elders do. They see crime and wickedness going on all around them; they never get a chance of knowing what goodness is. If only they could be taken out of their environment and educated, in a place something like a home *and* a school, from the time when they are little, why, then they would never grow up into cruel, lawless people, like so many of the adults.

"Some people, though, are doing their best to bring up their children to be decent citizens: they guide them at home and supervise their lives in a disciplined way; they send them to school and take an interest in what they are doing; they send them to church and to the church youth clubs, and all the family treat their priest as a friend and talk to him about their troubles. The children from broken homes, however, have a terrible time, they do not have the opportunity to have a good Christian upbringing, or to know what a secure family life is."

"Are these the ones you want to help?"

"No . . . there are some children—boys—even worse off than that."

And Mario knew that his innermost self had spoken at that moment.

"I want to help those most in need, those who suffer most, and I know that those who suffer most, of all the children of Naples, are . . . the Scugnizzi."

That was really what had been burning within him all those years, that was why he had felt that he could not settle down. He was not satisfied that he was a priest: he wanted to do the most he could, in the world; he wanted to help where he was *most* needed. To be a priest who was in charge of a parish might be all right for some, might be *their* life's work, but it was not his. It had not been enough for him. He had felt that he had to go out and take the Mass to those who *most* needed it—not to people who were already so religious that they would turn up anyway, but to factory-workers who had to get up so early that there just was no time for them to go to church before they started work. So it was with the children and the Youth Club; the boys in the Club were good boys from happy homes, and there were many young priests who were really fitted to look after them. There is always a place for everybody in life, and each one of us is "right" doing the job for which we are most fitted. Father Mario, therefore, wanted to look after those children who had no one else to look after them. Not even the children living in terrible conditions in broken homes were the ones *most* in need of care and love; no, it was the Scugnizzi who needed this; the Scugnizzi, whom he had known about since he was a boy and had seen in the dark alleys as he walked home from work in the barber's shop; the Scugnizzi, who

had increased in number during the War, when houses were demolished and families wiped out in the air-raids, when the black-market throve and all sorts of people got money illegally. Going about his tasks in the past three years, Mario had been always aware of this "other population" in the streets about him, and now he knew that it had pained him more deeply than he had imagined. He had only needed time to crystallise his thoughts. Now, suddenly, his thoughts *had* crystallised, and he knew that redeeming the Scugnizzi of Naples was to be his life's work.

"Oh Mario, that is a fine thought—that would be a splendid thing to do—but how *can* you help them? You know only too well how they go about in gangs, and how cruel they are. They would never join anything 'organised' like a Youth Club; anyway, they hate priests. Oh, it would be wonderful to be able to help them, but ... *how?*"

"Well, you remember how I made friends with the charcoal-burners because I was not dressed as a priest?"

"Yes?"

"I thought of something like that for the Scugnizzi. Actually . . ." and he blushed at having to reveal his deepest thoughts about the wonderful thing he had thought of doing, "I thought of dressing up in old, torn clothes, just like the ones they wear, and . . . sleeping out on the streets with them. I will have to keep my job at the school, of course, during the day; else what would I do for money? My mother relies on the money I give her for the housekeeping, and I don't want to sink to the level of real crime because I'm starving!" he chuckled. "They'll accept me in a gang, I hope, and I will be just like one of them and learn at first hand what it is really like to be a Scugnizzo. We were taught in the seminary to be like Christ. To be another Christ in the world would be impossible, but we can try to be like Him. He made friends with 'publicans and sinners', and when they asked Him why He did this He answered that He had come to call sinners to repentance. He was like a doctor, He said; and it is sick people, not healthy people, who need a doctor. That is why I want to go to the Scugnizzi: they are the sick who need a doctor. While I am with them I'll be getting to know what they are like, why they decide to take to the streets, their problems, fears, doubts, worries, hatreds and sins. In this way I'll know what is needed to help them, and I will pray to God for divine guidance as to how I can best help them. I do not know at this moment what that help can be, but in a few months' time I will know."

Father Ciccio looked at his friend with speechless admiration, but a shiver ran through him as he thought what Mario would have to go through before he achieved his aim.

"It will all be terribly dangerous; they might even . . . kill you!"

"I know. I have thought about all that. I have prayed. I know that this is the right thing to do. Christ taught us that we must love one another. There are few who can find it in their hearts to really love the Scugnizzi; most people hate them! I love them, that is all. If I go out to them, loving them, God will do the rest. As for the hardship that I will have to face, well, you know too, dear Ciccio, that nothing of lasting value and real good is ever achieved without suffering."

Father Mario was calm and nothing would deter him. Father Ciccio could hardly speak, he was so full of emotion at seeing the

48

inspired and dedicated state of his friend, but he managed to blurt out the words:

"I can't let you go alone, Mario—let me come with you!"

*   *   *

Mario was a priest, and priests cannot do things off their own bat, however inspired they may be. They belong to the Church and sometimes also to an "Order". A newly-ordained priest, especially, has to ask permission if he wants to do anything unusual. He has his superiors, and they must be obeyed. Father Ciccio wanted so much to help him, and he too asked for permission. Well, they both got the permission of their Bishop, who was very proud of them, but Father Ciccio could not convince the head of his Order that it was necessary for him to go out into the streets to redeem the Scugnizzi; he thought it could be done without actually identifying oneself with the toughs. Poor Father Mario! He felt quite alone. But he had told his plan to another friend of his, Salvatore, a photographer on one of the Naples daily papers. Salvatore was very enthusiastic about the idea, especially as, in the course of his work as a press photographer, he had seen often enough all the misery of the Scugnizzi's lives. So Salvatore took some pictures of them. Father Mario had asked him to. But they were not for the papers, they were for Father Mario to show to the Bishop

so that he would see how much need there was to do something for these boys. The photos showed them sleeping, mostly, because that was the only time *anyone* could take a photo of them, so wary were they of being recognised or caught. There they were, in the photos, all ragged; some wearing enormous boots many sizes too large for them, which they had stolen; some sleeping over bakers' shop gratings where warm air came up as the bread was being baked; and, in some photos, dogs, very thin, could be seen scavenging about near them for scraps of food; and in yet other photos rats could be seen. The Bishop's permission was more readily given because of these photographs.

This way of going about things shows how keen Father Mario was on using up-to-date methods in tackling his problems. He was a priest, but he was not going to let himself be bogged down by conventions of what a priest should say or do. That was obvious to everyone at this time.

CHAPTER 7

HIS BACK TO THE WALL

FATHER Mario stood with his back to the wall of an old grey building on one side of the Market Square—the Piazza Mercato. It was quite late, about ten o'clock at night and the Market Square was quite deserted. The barrows, however, were still there ranged along two sides of the square and the cold January wind tossed sheets of newspaper into the air to fly about in weird shapes like wild birds.

Refuse lay about too, rotten and squashed fruit and vegetables, the boxes and sacks in which they had been brought to market, cigarette butts.

Opposite him another similar building rose gaunt and sinister in the light of a single lamp which was affixed to the wall. At each corner of the square small streets disappeared into the unknown.

The whole place had a feeling of utter hopelessness.

Father Mario felt a shudder run through him as a fresh gust of wind howled down one of these side streets and gently lifted a pile of packing shavings and let them down again, only to pick them up with fresh vigour and roll them further back against the gutter. They looked like the frothy waves of some angry sea and seemed to Father Mario's nerve-racked mind to be part of the scene of hopelessness and despair.

He had on old clothes, the trousers tied at the ankles with string, and boots which were not even a pair. His jacket collar was pulled up against the cold and on his head he wore a large grimy cap. His face was so dirty that anyone would think that he had not washed for months and he certainly had not shaved for many days. His heart was pounding. He had said his prayers before he left and had dedicated his whole adventure to God like knights used to do in medieval times. Now he had to be like an actor living out his part as if he were in a play. He had to pretend that he was really a tough criminal and try to be accepted by a gang. If he failed he would be killed for certain.

He knew that a gang had their headquarters thereabouts and he knew roughly what the leader looked like, for he had taken the trouble to go about in the streets late at night finding out what sort of Scugnizzi were about.

Father Mario lounged against the wall, looking sinister. He had studied the attitude, expression and habits of the boys and he was doing his level best to look like one himself. Soon the gang-leader came strutting down one of the side-streets, pretending not to see him but, nevertheless, sauntering over and standing beside him. He spoke in a low voice.

"This is it!" thought Father Mario, and his heart was in his mouth.

"Who are you? I've seen you somewhere before!" said the gang leader.

"Oh well, I've been around . . . but . . ."

"Been anywhere near the prison lately?"

"I wouldn't like to be such a fool."

This gave the gang-leader the idea that Father Mario was on the run from the police, and that was just the idea he wanted him to have. In the gang-leader's mind this was quite a logical situation; this newcomer wanted to "go underground", to join a gang and so not be seen alone on the streets. Obviously he could not go back to the area where he had been before, because the police were looking for him. Another thing entered the leader's mind, however: this chap looked a really tough character; would he want to overthrow the leader, kill him probably, and then take charge of the gang himself? He had to keep on the right side of him or else . . .!

"Well, what's your name?"

"Mario."

"Fine! Mine's Carliucello. And we might as well understand each other straight away. Listen, this is *my* pitch, don't you come interfering here."

Father Mario made a terrific effort to force himself to think as if he were a Scugnizzo. He spoke gruffly, aggressively, as if he resented and mistrusted the other man. Any fear which showed in his face, any moment of thought about what he should do, would be interpreted as weakness by the other. Then in a flash he realised that he had to show not only that he was strong-minded but that he was stronger than the other. He really was with his back to the wall. It was do or die, him or the other. That was the law of the streets. The gang leader could not allow someone weaker than he in his area, and naturally thought that Father Mario felt the same about him. Quick as a flash, Father Mario sensed what he should do. He smartly put his hand inside his hip pocket and held it there as if it were on a knife; all the while he glowered at the gang-leader.

The situation was more than tense. The two men faced each other with an awesome do-or-die finality.

The gang-leader saw that he was beaten. *He* did not want to be killed. Better make friends—this Mario was obviously a tough character indeed. He jerked his head behind him.

"Better come and meet the gang."

The whole thing had been done with split-second timing. Few words had been exchanged. Father Mario secretly heaved a sigh of relief, but dared not show it. Instead, he scowled.

"All right, show me where they are. I might as well know."

He was glad now that he had not lost the fiery temper he had had since childhood. He had tried hard to keep it under control these last few years, but always it had flared up. Now he could use it to make up his new character.

Round the nearest corner, there they all were. Mario walked arrogantly over to them by Carliucello's side as if he didn't care much if he met them or not. When they got near enough Carliucello said:

"This is Mario. He's one of us from now on."

Most of the others stared up at him blankly but a small boy, who could not have been more than five, grinned up at him:

"Come and sit by me, Mario!"

As he did so, Mario realised that he was now a real Scugnizzo. He had to go all the way with them, he had to act the part completely. If they stole, would he have to steal? If they were unkind and cruel, would he have to do the same? He was still enough himself to abhor anything contrary to the teachings of Christ, and he felt that he could act well enough to seem to do these things without actually doing them.

There were about a dozen boys in the gang, all with odd nicknames like Mangy, Fatty, Whiskers, and Afoo. They were pulling cigarette stubs out of their pockets and opening them up with their thumb and forefinger, so making the tobacco still in the end fall out. This was carefully put onto a large piece of brown paper in the middle of the circle. Every boy was doing this and there was a veritable pile.

The fact that Scugnizzi picked up cigarette stubs in order to sell the tobacco to people who peddled it in the back streets had not

gone unnoticed by Mario, and he luckily had started off with a good supply of them in his pocket. So he quietly took his place in the circle and was soon indistinguishable from the rest.

They worked in silence with tired, drawn faces and occasionally one or other of them would steal a glance at the newcomer, wondering what he was like. The newcomer was, on his part, doing the same thing.

The boys he saw before him hardly seemed boys at all; nearly all of them were stunted in growth or deformed in some way or other. The one they called Mangy had a head too large for his body, covered with awful-looking hair. The smallest one, who had asked him to sit beside him, was called Nino. He was pitifully thin and his little hands, as they struggled to open the cigarette stubs, were like skeletons. Others had sad, all-knowing faces as if they were old men who had seen the most terrible things during their long, hard lives. Some had the faces of disillusioned men. None looked like the children they were. Their skins were grimy, their hands and nails black with dirt.

They all turned round as they saw a man approach. It was Salvatore.

He had a camera slung over his shoulder and walked towards them in a leisurely fashion. The Scugnizzi looked at him, but soon returned to their task, wondering who he was and what he would want of them.

"Well, hullo! Now this is an artistic scene! I wish my painter friend Arturo were here! He's always sketching and painting the scenes of Naples—sells them very well too. Mind if I sit down?"

The Scugnizzi didn't quite know how to take him but he seemed friendly enough and they were used to the art of summing people up. Mario, his powers of observation in operation to the highest degree, watched how they reacted, and treated Salvatore in the same way as they did.

Carliucello spoke: "I'm the leader of this gang. If you want to be our friend, you're welcome. Especially if you can bring us something to eat from time to time! (He raised a laugh from the others by this, and he was pleased with himself.) But if you start any funny business, put the police on us, or anything like that, well, my boys obey my commands without question and we'll—get rid of you—see?"

"Oh, my dear friends, I have no intention of doing anything to harm you, believe me! I'm a photographer, and my friends are all photographers or artists or musicians or the like and we know how hard life can be for those who don't conform to the usual ways of people. For instance, there are lots of people who wouldn't speak to me because I wear a casual sweater and my trousers aren't pressed! I ask you, have you ever heard of anything so absurd? I have one good suit which I wear when I go to see editors and people like that with photos for the papers. They speak to me then, take me out to coffee, or even to lunch at an expensive restaurant. But they wouldn't do that if I were dressed as I am now!"

The gang laughed. Mario laughed.

"Oh, I can see we are very much alike. We think the same things, feel the same way about people. Artists belong to a world of their own. We are not Rich People or Society People. We are not even Poor People, in the usual meaning of the word. We are part of everything and yet we are not a part of anything. We see people for what they are. Good is good. Bad is bad. Unkind is unkind. An evening among friends is an evening among friends." And with this he squatted down on the grimy, damp pavement beside them.

The Scugnizzi were full of admiration for him. Carliucello shook hands with him. He, like Mario, was accepted.

CHAPTER 8

THE COLDEST NIGHT

"'ERE, my lad, you come along with me!" Mario felt a large, strong hand clamping down on his shoulder.

"You belong to the Piazza Mercato Gang, you can't deny it, and your lot have done a very nasty job, stealing Army cigarettes and selling them. Tell me where the others are or I'll twist your arm."

Mario's eyes pleaded for compassion, but the policeman would have none of it.

"It's no use looking at me like that—I know who you are!" If only he did! thought Mario. If only he could tell! But he couldn't, because two or three of his companions were just around the corner all standing flat against the wall holding their breath, hoping not to be seen. The policeman did see them, however, and blew his whistle. Another two policemen appeared as if from nowhere and surrounded them.

Mario felt really a Scugnizzo at that moment. He had usually looked on the police as people with whom he could co-operate in keeping law and order, but now he felt like a trapped animal. He had grown very fond of his friends in the gang and had begun to realise that all their actions, their cunning way of carrying out robberies, their petty thefts of food and clothing, their self-assured, cocky, boastful and vain manner had all come about because they felt so alone in the world with no one to love or protect them. He had entered so fully into their lives that he felt all their emotions as if they were a part of him too, and at that moment, priest or not, he hated those policemen. Hated them, perhaps, more fully than the boys themselves because *they* were terrified of what might happen to them, but *he* was thinking how misguided these men were in treating boys cruelly. If they had had compassion and tried to understand the boys' behaviour, and to teach them new ways, the Scugnizzi would have had a whole army of good leaders and the policeman's work would have been admirable. As it was, their cruel attitude only fostered a rebellious attitude in the boys and made them hate mankind even more and feel even more that no one loved them at all.

Soon the police rounded them all up and took them to the police station. Mario kept silent. The policemen kept on hitting the boys from time to time and he got his full share. He thought—"People like these are so smarmy and polite when they talk to a priest—they are afraid, of course, because they are so wicked, that the priest will know somehow, and so they bow and say 'Yes, Father!' and 'Oh, quite so, Father!' and even kiss the hand of a priest. If only these policemen

knew that it is a priest they are hitting they would get a terrible shock!"

What you do to the least of these my Brethren, you do it unto Me. It seemed that the policemen had not heard these words. No one should ever be cruel to anyone at all—human being, animal or insect.

The policemen were being cruel to the Scugnizzi because they knew that they had no legal standing in the eyes of the law, they were not under the protection of their parents, they were "nobodies". The police would not have been so cruel if they had been boys from well-to-do homes! They would have told their fathers, who would have paid a lot of money to the police and all would have been well.

Very soon they were in the police station and all being interrogated and made to turn out their pockets. But part of the Scugnizzo's character is that he will be absolutely loyal to everyone within his gang, even to putting up with cruelty rather than blurting out any information, so the police could get nothing out of any of the boys. Father Mario kept silent. It was very difficult for him to be a Scugnizzo and yet still be true to himself as a priest. Not to steal, not to tell lies, and so on. If he had let the others see that he did not want to do these things they would have called him a softy and would have begun to wonder whether they should turn him out.

Very soon they were all let off with a caution ... "But wait till we catch any of you again!"

*   *   *

They trudged along the streets which were deserted and damp and very cold as it was January—frost skimmed the paving stones like Christmas cake icing, but the pavements were a very grim cake indeed. The idea of sleeping on the pavement tonight was definitely out!

"I know," said Afoo, "we could go to the bombed-out houses in the Maddalena district."

"O.K. You lead the way," said Carliucello.

They were all too tired to talk and the encounter with the police had upset them and made them edgy. That, and the cold atmosphere combined, made it seem that they were in a God-forsaken world. The little troupe struggled on past silent rows of tenements, up and

down many a winding alleyway. Even stray dogs had found shelter somewhere and were trying to get a few shivering hours of sleep. No one was about but these children, their ages ranging from four to fifteen—and Mario, the eldest. Little Nino was chattering with the cold as he was dragged along much faster than his baby legs could carry him.

"Hurry up, Nino." said one of the boys. But Mario picked him up and put him on his shoulder. As he felt the tiny baby hands around his neck Mario had a surge of anger again that anyone could be so heartless as to let such a defenceless little being go away from home and not bother about him. Bewilderment soon took the place of anger, however; how could people, he thought, stay indoors when they heard children roaming the streets on a night like this? How could richer people use their money to build villas on Capri or to buy fur coats when they knew there were hungry, ill-clad children out in the city without a roof over their heads? And how, oh how, could all these people go to church?! A prayer for help went up from the depths of his heart, but it was not the prayer of someone who prays for others, he was not an onlooker, he was part of it all.

"Dear God, don't forsake us!" he secretly prayed.

Soon they reached an area of bombed-out houses and made for the inside of one of them. There were bits of wood and rubbish lying around and they found enough of this to light a fire, but they had to keep it low because, if the police saw them . . .

Nino and the younger ones sat around the fire shivering while the others collected the drier scraps of wood and burnable material and set light to it. Then they tried to bank it up a bit so that it would keep in an hour or two and make them all warm. There was nothing to eat, so they all lay down and went to sleep, close to each other for warmth, some with their heads on another's back, using it as a pillow, and yet another head on *their* back!

Mario was most uncomfortable and could not sleep straight away, but he did not show this as the others would realise he was not used to this method of sleeping! Before he dropped off he let his mind wander over the things he had learnt about the Scugnizzi. Loving care as was normally found in a home was the real need but the hunger which gnawed relentlessly at his empty stomach told him that food was perhaps next on the list of their needs. Because of the night's happenings, however, two new things were obvious needs: warmth, body-warming clothes, the drying heat of a fire; and a dry, cosy place to sleep in with a roof to keep the elements out—walls were a secondary consideration. These first things were the minimum that anyone could need in order just to keep alive. It was for these things that the gangs roamed about stealing and doing odd jobs. If they could be given these things they would have no need to be Scugnizzi any more. They only led a life of crime in order to survive.

This was the beginning of his knowledge of how to help them — God was answering his prayers. If the boys could have a *home*, a building with a real roof, rooms, a place for each one to sleep, even if only a palliasse on the floor, a stove where someone could cook their meals, a fire to warm themselves by, but above all a place where lived someone who *cared* for them, they would cease their bad ways of living and become normal, happy children once more.

Mario fell asleep visualising such a home where *he* would be the someone who cared.

CHAPTER 9

THE CHURCH AND THE ORANGES

"LET'S go in here." It was Mangy who spoke.

"In here?" Mario asked contemptuously. They were in a cool side street where a dry, worm-eaten but beautifully-carved ancient door showed that they were in front of a church. Mario had an awful feeling in the pit of his stomach—a church! A part of his real life! How pleased he would have been if they had wanted to go in there to pray or to hear him say Mass! He couldn't let them see any of this, however. He had to show that, like them, he could not bear the sight of the inside of a church. But why did they want to go in? He was curious to know.

Mangy, with his pitifully dirty hair and head covered in sores, pushed open the door very deftly, because it might have creaked a little. He held it open only a slit so that the others could slide through and looked back at them with an expression in his eyes which said "You all know you have to be quiet" and held up a grimy forefinger to his lips. They quietly slid in. Almost choking with emotion, Mario followed. It was almost unbearable for him not to be able to make the sign of the cross or bow to the altar, but he managed to turn an intense gaze towards the altar and think a prayer.

"What they are going to do, dear Lord, I do not know, but please watch over them and make me help You!"

"Quick, out all of you, they've heard us!" Carliucello exclaimed, and in a flash they were all out again in the street and running for dear life! Mario ran too, but he did not know why they all ran, or what had happened.

They ran and ran, almost a mile it seemed, and at last, breathless, they all stopped as Carliucello had given the sign. They were on a bomb site, out of view of any house, where some tall hoardings screened them from the road. The bombed buildings were not all razed to the ground; some parts still stood and, as this place had become a dumping-ground for any old thing, the Scugnizzi had in the past discovered some planks and had made a rough shelter where they often came with their spoils. They made for this shelter now. Carliucello beckoned them all in and the boys squatted as best they could among the rubble of broken bricks and plaster.

They formed a rough ring round Mangy and all waited expectantly. Mario, crouching with the others, craned his neck to see what Mangy was doing. Glancing furtively around, just to make sure no one was looking, even in that hideout, Mangy drew from under his arm something which he had held tightly concealed under his jacket. It was a church alms-box.

"So that was why they wanted to go into the church," thought Mario. "It's terrible! They are only children and this is what they have sunk to, stealing money which people, poor themselves, have given in order to help those even poorer." The church had been in a very poor district indeed and he had often said Mass in similar churches. The people were good, honest folk who tried to scrape a living. They had tired, weary faces, lined with years of privation and suffering. As they filed out after Mass, some of them, usually the older women, dressed in patched black dresses and black head-scarves, would rummage in their purses and put a coin or two in the box. It was a real sacrifice, for those coins were needed to pay the rent, buy food, or oil for their lamps.

"How much?" they nearly all asked, eagerly, as Mangy counted out the coins.

"Twenty pence," he answered in a flat tone. There was disappointment but not anger among the boys. "We can buy some charcoal for our fire to-night," said one.

"Hand the money over," said Carliucello. "Right! Afoo, here's eighteen pence—go and buy a packet of charcoal. Tommaso," he grinned, "here's tuppence—you know how to stretch that and 'buy' us some fruit!"

They all laughed raucously. "I wonder, what are they up to now?" thought Mario.

*   *   *

Tommaso grabbed the twopence.

"Watch me!" he said.

He walked calmly down one of the streets and then another, while the rest of the gang followed him warily at a distance. No one should know that they were something to do with him. At last they approached a small square where street vendors were shutting up their stalls for the night. There was not much fruit because it was February —a few apples and oranges was about all. Tommaso went straight to the vendor at one of the stalls, a man with a rotund and jovial figure. He was all muffled up in an enormous coat, threadbare scarf and hat, and on his hands was an old pair of gloves with the fingers cut off so that he could easily handle money while still keeping warm.

"Any unsound fruit you can't sell?" Tommaso enquired, in the sweetest of voices.

"Well, you can have this, and this, and this," said the man, picking up from the gutter some bruised apples as quickly as his figure would let him. "There you are, son." He was a kindly man and did not like to see this little boy obviously hard-up at home go away empty-handed.

"Oh, *thank* you, sir!" Tommaso's voice was over-polite as he pushed the slimy fruit into his tattered pockets.

Detecting, perhaps, a slightly wicked gleam in the boy's eyes, the man thought it about time to be rid of him. "There's nothing more! Be off with you!"

"Er . . . please," stammered Tommaso, "I've . . . got a little money, my mother said you'd be kind and give me the best you can for it."

Oh, what a terrible thing it was, to be sure, to have little money, thought the man, "I'll try to help where I can."

"What about this orange? It's a big one, fivepence is the price of one as large as that. How much money have you?"

"Only tuppence," said a very dejected little boy. "Only tuppence."

"All right, you can have it for tuppence!" The vendor spoke gruffly, but his warm heart had won and showed through his voice and gave him away. This revelation of his character was not lost on Tommaso, who had been weighing him up all the time. Knowing that the man would be indulgent towards him, he took the orange in his hands, turned it round lovingly and felt its weight, then eyed another one—

"Can't I have that one over there? It's a bit bigger. It would go farther at home, my baby brother would be able to have some too, as well as my little sister."

The man was amused, and also wrung with compassion for this poverty-stricken family, but he felt that giving away one orange cheap was quite enough for the present. Later, when he got to know the family better, he could let them have all sorts of things, but just now there was something about the boy which did not inspire trust. One fruit was enough but, just to satisfy the boy that he had given him the largest orange he had, he let him hold the second orange in his other hand.

"There! You can see it's no bigger. Feel the weight of the two. *You'll* never make a fruit merchant if you can't tell quicker than that which is the bigger and heavier of two oranges!" he chuckled.

Just out of sight, in a side street, the gang waited, watching Tommaso's every move. Mario wondered what it was all about.

Suddenly Tommaso dropped the two oranges deftly, smartly, straight down to the ground, and in a trice kicked them backwards

with his heels. They whizzed towards the others who, quick as lightning, picked them up and ran for their lives.

The vendor was so surprised that he hardly knew what had happened and he was far too fat to be able to chase them. That was why Tommaso had chosen him and not the other vendors.

Mario hardly knew what had happened, either, as he ran yet again with the others to get away from a wrongdoing.

That night there was fruit to eat for all, in front of a warm fire.

"Thou shalt not steal," Mario thought.

When they had finished their meal—bread stolen by Whiskers from the back door of a bakehouse while the baker was serving in the shop, the fruit stolen by Tommaso, some cheese which had fallen off a van as it trundled through the cobbled streets, coffee made

in their billy-can from old coffee grounds out of a hotel dustbin—
they made off for the night. Walking a little distance, they came across
a silent street. It was past midnight and they were all so tired. One of
the houses had an entrance archway and under it they crept and all
fell asleep.

They had not been there more than an hour when one of the men
who went to work early came down the staircase. He was furious at

finding them all there and kicked them with his heavy boots. "Be off
with you or I'll call the police." The boys knew he meant this and they
got up and went away, shouting a few rude things at him as they went.

Mario, in no mood to be pushed about, and really ill through lack
of sleep and all his weeks on the road, shouted at him too, but he
was still his old self enough to say: "Do unto others as you would
like others to do to you!" The man picked up a stone and threw it at
him.

Mario thought: there were too many people about only ready to
chase them away from the streets, not caring if they lived or died,
not wanting them to exist, but not bothering to wonder why they
were on the streets at all. Not caring enough for them to give them
some food or a place to sleep in. No one cared about them, no one
would stick up for them, and certainly no one would ever shield
them from harm. If anyone was ever unkind or cruel to the Scugnizzi

—and many often were—people only said: "Serve them right!" or "They deserve it!" and things like that. The people around were full of unkindness and real cruelty—of course the Scugnizzi had to defend themselves or they would starve to death. When they left home, they had to invent a completely new personality just in order to be able to survive on the streets. They became more like hunted animals than human beings.

"Seeing people around them so cruel, they see all of life as a cruel thing where the Law of the Jungle is the only law," thought Mario. "No one is around to show, by his example, that such things as 'Love thy neighbour as thyself' have ever been thought about."

This, Mario knew, was *his* task, and, gradually, he began to let them see that he was a kind person.

CHAPTER 10

AN HONEST PENNY

It is not the beginning of the work, but the continuing of the work, until it is thoroughly finished, that yieldeth the true glory.

IN the evenings, after school and before going to the Piazza Mercato, Mario could sometimes steal away to the Youth Club. Other young priests had filled the gap he had left but it was still his Club. The aftermath of war had brought a tide of boys to youth clubs all over Italy, eager to replace the remembered Fascist regime and German occupation with constructive work and well-informed study which would reform and build a new Italy. These clubs were organised by the Church through the Vatican, and had even kept going during the War, thanks to Mgr. Montini who afterwards became Pope Paul in 1963. Many of the boys were in their late teens while others were young men in their early twenties. Hearing of Father Mario's work among the Scugnizzi, the members of these clubs all over Naples, including the ones at the Materdei Club, went as much as they could to Materdei to hear about Father Mario Borrelli's work, hoping to be there on the evenings on which he would drop in. Then they would gather round him and listen with the greatest enthusiasm as he would tell them in the strictest confidence, of course, about his hours on the streets. They would all stay on, discussing and talking about the problems of Naples in 1950, but, when the clock's hands approached ten, he would take his leave of them to prepare for his evening's work.

Father Mario would then make his way through the streets which he knew like the back of his hand and eventually reach an old monastery where he would go in through the arched doorway, go up the stairs to one of the cells, and enter it. A friend of his who was a monk there, had given him the use of his cell as a changing-room. To the people at Materdei, although they knew of his work, he had been a priest, dressed in the usual way for a priest to be dressed, to the people along the road, whom he passed, Scugnizzi included, he was just another of the many priests who walked around Naples. From his parish to his church, perhaps, then, this priest would be seen going into the monastery but who would trouble to wait outside to see when he came out?

While he was in his friend's cell, a strange transition took place, not only did he put on all the ragged, dirty clothes which he wore on the streets, but he also had to put on a new personality, he had to leave his own personality behind with his soutane! He was now an actor, he was acting the part of someone with a hard outlook on life, someone who was more inclined to hate than to love, to be cruel than to be kind, to be lawless rather than law-abiding, who scoffed at the Church and all it stood for, but he was doing all this just because he himself was the opposite to all these things.

After this transition had taken place he left his friend's cell and went down the staircase. Then, out on the road, he became "Mario the Scugnizzo" and slouched along the road in his nightly role, ready to spend another almost sleepless night on the streets of his native city.

* * *

Carliucello said one evening, "I know what we'll do tonight, we'll earn an honest penny," then he laughed his horrible guffaw of a laugh. "We'll go to the Via Carracciolo, where the hotels are and open car doors for people as they go out for the evening. I saw a poster outside the San Carlo Opera House, the winter season for opera is still on and so we should be able to earn quite a bit in tips. Mario, you go and Whiskers and Afoo, you all know what to do, of course, just run and open the car door as the person comes out of the hotel, be very polite, give a little bow, and shut it gently when they are in but take care to put your hand out for the money before you shut the door."

Accordingly, the three of them went along to this wide road on the sea-front and hovered around one of the big hotels. The hotel had a very smart entrance and an impressive flight of steps led down to the road, for, wishing to dissociate the people who stayed at the hotel from the "riff-raff of the streets" the designers had decided to put the main floor not on ground level but on the first floor. Down this flight of steps well fed and overweight Neapolitan women of the millionaire class came bouncing down, dressed in the latest fashion in dinner-dresses and very high-heeled shoes into which their fat legs were poured seemingly to end in a point. Nothing less than a mink stole was on their shoulders, of course! Long American Cadillacs drew up smoothly with press-button precision managing to arrive at the foot of the steps at the precise moment that the millionaire ladies reached them!

Mario, Afoo and Whiskers stood at a distance observing all this keenly and working out in their minds what would be the precise moment for them to leap forward and smartly open the car door, thus earning a reward of a few *soldi*.

A car drew up, driven by a well-dressed but greasy-looking man in a pale grey suit. Mario moved swiftly to the door of the car just as a small, fat lady wearing a tight black dress, a lot of jewellery and a short, black, Persian lamb coat, came sweeping down the steps, followed immediately by a smartly-uniformed commissionaire. Mario opened the door with a flourish and a bow and, at the same time, held out his hand for a tip. The commissionaire was very cross indeed, but with his smart uniform and white gloved hands he disdained to hit the offending ragamuffin. He satisfied himself by saying "Be off, or I'll call the police!" The fat lady got into the car as quick as she could and shut the door herself with a bang heedless of his hand on the door-handle, giving him a push as she entered. Mario, angry, not for what she had done to him but because people existed who *could* be so hard as not to be moved by compassion at seeing a hungry, ragged, homeless boy, looked at her heavily made-up face and tried to fathom what her soul really was like. He saw it as only a dark place.

Meanwhile, inside the car, the Rich Lady was having the jitters.

"How nauseating! One of those filthy urchins actually stood near *me*. I think those sort of people should be behind bars or in an approved school, or something, what *are* the Police doing nowadays? I must talk to Giorgio about it and see if he can do anything about it when next he goes up to Parliament." Then she glanced at her diamond braceleted watch.

"Oh *do* hurry, Carlo, the First Act of the Opera begins in two minutes! Oh! One of those filthy beings is giving me a really nasty look. Oh! I can't bear it. Let's get away . . . quick . . . he looks as though he wants to kill me! Those eyes, they seem to be accusing me of something." The car lurched forward and the Rich Lady soon forgot all about the accusing eyes as her senses were swathed in the soothing and amusing tunes of Donizetti's music. But the eyes, the accusing eyes, were not the eyes of a ragamuffin, they were the eyes of a priest! If only she had known, she would not have slept easily that night and, in the morning, she would perhaps have hung one of her less expensive necklaces round the neck of the papier-mâché Madonna in her local church and would have thought that this act could make Christ forgive her for her lack of compassion.

There are a few rich ladies in Naples who do not act like this, instead they "feed the hungry, clothe the poor, comfort the comfortless, visit the sick" but they really are very few indeed, there are far too many like that Rich Lady

Round the back of the hotel, where the garages were, two of the others were hanging about. When people came in with their cars they would ask whether they wanted it washed; *sometimes* the answer would be "Yes", in this way they really did manage to earn "an honest penny". Mario was quick to notice this and learned from it that the Scugnizzi would only stoop to dishonesty because they could not find any honest job as no one would trust them. Yet they longed to get away from their inferior station in life and eagerly searched for jobs. In the summer, he knew, many of the Scugnizzi worked for the men who hired rowing boats or arranged trips on pleasure-steamers and then they stood on the quay shouting for customers. In this way they could spend a few months in comparative security . . . and be able to eat a pizza or two a day with the proceeds! Also, waiting at the station and offering to carry people's attache cases was another honest way of earning money. Sometimes people didn't want their cases carried though! Another way of earning an honest penny was to sell picture postcards of Naples along the front.

One night, after the usual work of stealing, climbing up people's balconies, entering their flats and stealing the washing off the lines which jutted out at right angles to the building, they were all walking along looking for somewhere to sleep.

It seemed to Mario that they were always walking, and it was quite true. Far into the night they walked, looking for a place to sleep, being sent away by someone, and having to find another place; the little ones getting dragged along, whimpering, half asleep.

On they walked, and, tired as he was, Mario still noticed that Giulio, who was in front of him, was wearing a very threadbare jacket indeed, and he wondered how the boys managed to get their clothes. He did not have to wonder long, however, because in an alleyway they came across the prone figure of an American soldier. He was fast asleep and snoring.

"He's drunk!" said Giulio contemptuously, then looked, a very knowing look, at Whiskers. "What about it, eh?"

All the boys immediately set to work at taking the G.I.'s clothes off him, shoes, socks, jacket, trousers, underclothes, everything. Carliucello supervised the work, and himself took the wallet.

"Come on, boys, let's go!"

Mario, who always tried not to actually *do* any of the crimes, had stood a little apart and watched out, ready to give the alarm. As the boys took each article of clothing off they handed it to him, and now he found himself holding a bundle of khaki and white clothing. He glanced at the G.I., still lying there, dead-drunk. As a priest, and a Christian, how could he leave him there? He, Mario, was acting the part of the thieves in the story of the Good Samaritan. If he showed the gang he was against this, however, they would surely get rid of him, kill him off, for he knew now too many of their secrets. And although he was brave enough to face that and fight back, he knew he must not give up. That would be the end of his mission, he would not be able to help them, teach them and give them a home. So, reluctantly, he followed Carliucello who was already getting suspicious and very impatient as he waited at the entrance to another dark alley.

"Getting cold feet? It's too late now, if the police find us! We must get this stuff sorted out. Come *on*!" It was too far to walk back to

their hideout on the bomb site but Carliucello knew all the streets like the back of his hand.

"There's a Largo just at the end of this alley with an old fountain in it. The buildings there are warehouses mostly, so no one will see us. We can go there."

In the farthest corner of the Largo in an old crumbling archway Carliucello told Mario to put the clothes down.

"Now, Giulio, you can have the tunic, you need one," said Carliucello. Mario was pleased about this and he handed the jacket to Giulio.

"Does anyone else need anything?" asked Carliucello.

"I'd like the vest!" said Tino, as he fingered it with his grimy hands. It looked like real silk.

Carliucello's hand came down on his with a heavy slap. "I didn't say you could have it! I asked if anybody *needed* anything, and you *don't*. You stole one off someone's line only three months ago, remember?"

Tino looked longingly at the vest—he had *so* wanted it.

Mario, watching, was filled with compassion. He saw in Tino just a little boy. He was only about seven, wanting something as children usually do when they look into shop windows—but usually their mother is there and she tries to buy the thing for them.

He bent over towards Tino: "It's far too large for you, really," he smiled. "One day, perhaps, you'll have one just your size, all for yourself, even if I have to buy it for you!"

"Yes, that's right," said Carliucello. "One day, things will be looking up and we'll all have tons of money"—and he laughed, a bitter, mocking laugh.

"O.K. All the other clothes I'll take myself to the old-clothes dealer who has his barrow in the Market Place. He never asks where things come from and I know how to beat a good bargain."

A church clock struck five as they bundled the tell-tale khaki into a piece of tarpaulin which they had found in the alley way, and Carliucello discussed the day's plans with the others. He himself, after selling the clothes, would throw the wallet into a fire which the people in the shanty-town lit to burn up rubbish, and the money would go into his pocket. He would use some of it to buy contraband cigarettes and then they would sell these and even start a little back-street business. Luck was in that day. The others told him what they were going to do and they all agreed to meet again somewhere around the Piazza Mercato that evening.

73

Mario, dizzy and dropping with exhaustion, slowly walked to the fountain which was dripping icy water into a cracked black stone basin and washed. Then he said good-bye, and went towards the trams.

"Mario never tells us what he does during the day, but *I* know," said Carliucello, "I've seen him board a tram—he picks people's pockets and steals their wallets—it's so easy when there's a rush-hour crush. I'll do it myself one day."

But Mario the Scugnizzo got off the tram a long way away from the poor quarter and changed back into his soutane and went off to say Mass, as he did every morning. Then he had some coffee and a roll and went to teach at the school.

It was 9.30 when he eventually reached the headmaster's room to sign on for the day. "I'm sorry I'm late," he murmured.

"All right, my son," said the Prior, "But, remember, don't overdo things."

Mario, frightened, thinking the Prior had guessed what he was doing and would reveal his secret and spoil everything, looked at him in horror.

"Your class is waiting."

"Yes. Of course!"

An unshaven priest, coming in late! What an example to the boys! What *does* he do at night? thought the Prior.

As Mario started teaching, Carliucello was down by the docks.

A ship was coming into the harbour as he lounged idly against a capstan. He was half-smiling and seemed to be viewing the pleasant scene but his alert eyes, narrowed to slits against the light, were searching for any movement from the portholes. Soon enough, something did happen. A small, greyish bag appeared at one of them and was being pushed out. It landed with a soft bounce on the water's surface and gently floated with the tide.

Carliucello's eyes showed a satisfaction, but not complete satisfaction. They were still waiting for something and turned their intense gaze on another area, scanning the small space of shadowed water between the side of the ship and the harbour wall. Soon this search too, was rewarded and Carliucello's head nodded a little, knowingly, while his eyes expressed approval. A small rowing boat had appeared from inside the harbour, as from nowhere, and the boatman kept his oars still and seemed to be idling there, waiting to help the sailors anchor the boat, perhaps. The grey bag rose and fell with the gently lapping water. And the boatman was beside it, hardly having seemed

to move towards it. And now it was in his boat, though no one, however observant, could have noticed.

Carliucello's eyes showed approval. The boatman moved off silently. Carliucello waited a few more minutes, lounging there still studying the boat, slit-eyed, and yet a lingering smile on his lips.

Then he stretched, yawned and slouched off along the quayside in the direction which the boat had taken. He seemed to be sauntering along, taking a stroll, but, as ever, his alert eyes had the edge of the quay always in view. Eventually he stopped, lit a cigarette, and sat on a stone. His eyes took in everything that was going on. Lorries and cars and trams were speeding along the wide road behind him, but at this part of the quayside there was no bustle, only two men walking to or from some job or other.

One of them was carrying a small grey bag. He walked behind a bunker which was placed between where Carliucello was sitting and the water's edge. He seemed to stoop, slightly, as he passed behind it and when he re-appeared he was still carrying a small grey bag but Carliucello knew that it was not the same one he was carrying before!

The man crossed the road, winding his way expertly in and out of the stream of traffic. Carliucello saw that when he reached the other side, he went up a certain street.

During the morning he went up that same street himself and came to a warehouse which seemed unused. He pushed open the old wooden door and walked up a grey stone staircase to a room on the first landing.

A short, squat man of about fifty in a worn, oily, brown striped suit was sitting at a desk facing the door; he greated Carliucello as he entered.

"Well! What do *you* want?"

"Got any work for me?"

"No! Not for *you*—you can't even pay for the goods."

Carliucello smiled. He pulled from his pocket a wad of dollars which he had found in the G.I.'s wallet.

"How's that? Can we talk business now?"

The man's eyes boggled. "Where did you get that?"

"Never you mind!"

"How many do you want?"

"Say 50 to start with."

The man went to a cupboard behind him and opened it with a key he took from a chain round his waist. Inside the cupboard was a grey bag. Carliucello permitted himself a smile.

The man took out fifty packets of American cigarettes from the bag and Carliucello asked how much this would cost. He bargained with the man and eventually they settled on a lower price.

Before he left the room, Carliucello had hidden all the cigarettes. He tied a piece of string which the man gave him around the ankles of his baggy trousers and pushed most of the packets down the trouser legs. Others he put inside his shirt, then buttoned his jacket very tightly. Soon he was making for the hideout on the bomb site.

He carefully piled all but twelve packets in a corner of the hideout and covered them with the piece of tarpaulin. Then he hid ten of the remaining twelve in his shirt and put one packet in each of his jacket side-pockets, and walked back to the streets near the Piazza Mercato.

The Piazza was a bustle of activity, as it was about midday. Housewives were buying food, and business men and sailors and soldiers went among the stalls, buying and looking at the wares displayed.

Carliucello stood in one of the side-streets, just a few feet from the entrance to a coffee bar. As men passed him he looked carefully at them. If they seemed fairly poor and also not likely to give him away, he whispered: "Cigarettes ... American ... very good ... very cheap ..." If anyone stopped, he whispered the price, which was cheaper than the shop price. Then the buyer paid him and he handed over the packet, making it all as little obvious as possible.

How proud Carliucello was that night.

"Well! I'll soon be leaving you lot to fend for yourselves. With that money the G.I. so kindly *gave* me I think I can set up a business. I've made quite a lot of money to-day." And he told them how he had begun to sell contraband cigarettes.

Mario understood from this that the Scugnizzi were only too ready to better themselves and take a step up in the world, even if that step led only to the hand-to-mouth living of a business in smuggled goods. He also realised that he could help them if he could find jobs for them which were legal instead of illegal. They would be pleased to find themselves becoming "respected citizens".

But he also realised, with an awful sinking feeling, that he would have to hurry up and find them the "home" before any of them, as Carliucello was doing, started to grow out of just being Scugnizzi and settled down into more grown-up forms of crime.

CHAPTER 11

DESPAIR ... AND HOPE

NIGHT after night, month after month, Mario went through these harrowing experiences, and even more harrowing ones still. He began to feel very ill and terribly exhausted and in this state he began to know real despair, as he had already known the beginnings of hate. Truly, he had become almost a Scugnizzo himself, for these were some of the very things that he had dedicated himself to "curing" in the Scugnizzi. In becoming so completely identified with the Scugnizzo character he had drunk the dark cup of knowledge of them to the very dregs. He *knew* beyond any doubt what they were really like. It was truly a mystical "Sacrifice", akin, in a way, to the Sacrifice he offered every morning in the Mass. Only through the intense suffering of his life in the streets, only by losing his whole personality and becoming as a Scugnizzo and feeling nearly the same hate and despair which made them what they were, could he attain the summit of his strivings and know what to do for them. This in itself was Christlike for Christ came down to earth as an ordinary human being and suffered as human beings suffer in order to be able to say "I know what you all have to go through, I have endured it all Myself." Some people wonder why Christ "had to die for us". They feel that, at the last moment, Angels could have come and saved Jesus from the Cross. But I myself feel that the Crucifixion had to be endured by Christ because it was just the sort of thing that would happen to an ordinary human being, because that is just how cruel human beings are to each other; and by going through all that, Christ could be forever near all those who suffered in any way because He had suffered so much in the deepest suffering that could be.

When great suffering comes our way, we must be ready to accept it and to descend to the depths of suffering, as in this way we can help others. But we can only do this if we surmount our suffering. It was no use for Mario just to suffer with the Scugnizzi, he had to find a solution to their problems from within himself, from his vocation as a priest, and lift them out of their suffering. Some people, when they have gone through some unhappy experience, such as a serious illness or the unkindness of others, feel that they have "found themselves". They learn that life is not just amusing oneself or having a good time but a serious time which we can use to the best advantage by using our talents for the good of our fellow men. They learn also that many suffer in life, and many need to be helped, and that people are happier bringing comfort to others than when

they think only of earning money in order to be able to buy things for their own selfish pleasures.

Now Mario was walking down the street to the Piazza Mercato. Whenever he saw a cigarette end on the ground he stooped to pick it up and put it in his pocket. He had grown so accustomed to this that it had become second nature to him, yet the very act of doing it made him feel low-spirited, as if he were a person who had sunk so low in the world that the only way he could make money was from the things that others had finished with. He felt very depressed and . . . it was cold!

Turning the corner he saw, across the square, in the grey light of the oncoming dusk, his gang, sitting in a circle. They were sorting out their cigarette butts as on the first night he had met them all. And no wonder they persisted in this. Many people, even those who were not Scugnizzi, made about six shillings a day by selling the tobacco from the ends. It was the boys' chief, steady income; and it was, at least, honest! Their faces were apathetic, hopelessness seemed to have taken hold of them, they slouched dejectedly . . . and

79

he knew exactly how they felt. He stood for a while gazing at them, thinking about them.

There was Nino, the smallest, hunched up against the cold, a small grey silhouette. He was so very thin, how could he survive the rigours of this existence much longer? He was always shivering and coughing. Mario wanted to pick him up in his arms and carry him away from

all this, buy him some medicines and cure him of the cough and then keep him warm and cared for in a loving home.

Then, at the other end of the scale, was Carliucello, the eldest, almost seventeen, yet this life had caused him to grow into a stocky, stunted youth. Mario thought of the boys he taught during the day, in their teens, full of the excitement of growing up, their healthy bodies developed by games like football and tennis, their young minds expanding day by day as they learned to explore new fields of thought, and were taught to use their lives for the good of mankind. The Scugnizzi, instead, had no teachers, they were like wild animals at bay and only their animal instincts flourished. Their minds did not expand but became stunted, like their bodies. They had irrational fears, their minds created a strange world where terrors lurked which they had never known and which did not exist. When a person is very optimistic and full of enthusiasm and the joy of living, people say that person is "seeing the world through rose-coloured spectacles": meaning that everything looks to that person prettier and nicer than it really is. The Scugnizzi were just the opposite, they seemed to be seeing the world through grey-tinted spectacles. People, buildings, animals, the sea, the streets, everything they saw or thought, was seen and thought about in quite a different way from their "brothers" who were not Scugnizzi. When each of them had left home he had been, even if neglected and maltreated, still a child. This life had changed them all until now they were more like men, not ordinary normal adult men, but hunted men like escaped prisoners.

It seemed unbelievable to Mario, at that moment, that of all the educated adults in Naples, no one, no doctor, teacher or politician, no priest, lawyer or councillor, no one at all had been appalled at the sight and thought of these unhappy creatures who hardly knew why they did what they did and certainly did not understand what was happening to them. The only people, it seemed, who were aware of the Scugnizzi's plight and cared enough to try to alleviate their misery were the Salvation Army, thought Mario, for had he not himself, several times, with the gang, gone to their stall and been given free cocoa and bread? They were indeed to be praised.

He gazed across at the darkening group, realising that this was one of those rare moments when life seems to stop, when there is no need to pray because the very moment *is* a prayer. God is very near and makes us know, in those moments, what he wants us to do. Mario saw quite clearly then that he had to find the boys a real home straight away. He was the one person who had dedicated his life to the task of helping them. Now he knew enough about them, their needs, wants and all their complex character, to be able to prepare a new way of life for them. He knew that they needed food, shelter, warmth, clothing, medical care. He also knew they needed to be shown that kind people do exist in the world. If honest work could be found for them they would rather do it than dishonest work because they longed to be respected as decent human beings. He knew too, however, that no Scugnizzo would ever go to any place Mario might have ready for them because he was told, or even asked, to go; a Scugnizzo would only go if he felt he was going because he himself was curious to know what the place was like!

Slowly he walked across the square to them, not completely able to put his thoughts aside, not able to revert instantly to his role of Scugnizzo. He gazed at the group, in a half dream, thinking: "They are my boys, my companions, how I love them..."

The boys turned round as he came towards them and the things he was thinking showed in his eyes as they rested on all of them.

"Mario! Mario!" Their greeting was full of bewilderment as somehow they sensed that there was something out of the ordinary about him. They felt comforted and more hopeful because he was with them.

CHAPTER 12

THE BEGINNINGS OF A HOME

THE very next day he got in touch with the Church authorities and told them he was looking for a building somewhere to make a home for the Scugnizzi. Was there a disused church somewhere? "Oh, well," came the answer, "Why not that little church—what is it called?—oh, yes—Materdei." Mario gasped, but hid his surprise. Had they forgotten that they had already given him Materdei as Youth Club? Best say nothing or else they might take the offer away. He accepted.

He was very light of heart when he next went to Materdei. After months of not really knowing where he was, not being quite sure what form the help he could give the Scugnizzi might take, he had something definite. The building would be used as the home for the Scugnizzi. He told Ciccio, and one other young priest, and the older boys who all agreed that they would become his helpers and would start getting Materdei ready. How excited they were!

Mario explained to Vittorio and Pasquale how he had discovered the things the Scugnizzi needed through being one of the gang. Vittorio was a young schoolteacher who was helping to get Materdei ready, Pasquale was another friend. "So we'll need to find them a place to sleep, that's the first important thing. There are eight in the gang.... Of course, we won't be able to buy eight beds! And anyway, if we did, they wouldn't know what to do with them, so used are they to just lying down on the ground."

"Well, we'd better just clear out a room, keep it dry and put down something for them to sleep on, straw perhaps."

"Yes, but straw would get awfully dirty and we'd have to change it."

"What about straw mattresses, then?"

"What a splendid idea! Ciccio, you are so practical. I don't know what I'd do without you," said Mario. "The boys from the Youth

Club will, I'm sure, willingly sew up some sheeting into large mattress bags and we can get some straw from the market and fill them."

"But, Mario! Where is the money coming from to buy these things, and the other things you'll need later?"

Mario was happy and nothing could dampen his ardour. "Some of my friends have said they'll give a bit of money for this and also, well, I've learned a lot about buying and selling 'rags-and-bones', old clothes, junk, while I've been on the streets . . . I'll turn myself— and all of you who are willing to help me—into rag-and-bone men. We can go from house to house asking for things and then, when we have them, we can sell them in the various markets. That way we can really begin to keep house. Here's something from my wages this week—I'd like you to get some medical supplies with it. Nino is terribly ill, he needs penicillin, and some of the others too need one or two things; here's a list."

"Very well, Mario," said Vittorio, "I'll do my best for you. We can clear up the place and stay here, sleep here ourselves, and in that way the moment you decide to bring the boys here, you can. We will be ready to welcome them at a moment's notice; we'll always have some food ready, even if it's only a little."

And Vittorio went off to organise the helpers into getting the place ready, and starting the rag-and-bone business. But Mario went back to his gang.

*   *   *

Mario could hardly go through with his Scugnizzo act any longer, now that he knew Ciccio and Vittorio were getting Materdei ready for them. How would he tell them, he wondered. It would be more than terrible to spoil everything by saying: "I'm not a Scugnizzo, I'm a priest. I've done all this because I wanted to find out what you needed. And now I know, I've got a house with some food and shelter for the night." No, he would have to be more careful than that. He would have to say, somehow, that there was a place where one could go for the night, opened up by some kind people; then, if the Scugnizzi wanted to go there, *he* would have to go into Materdei with them, as if he were really one of the gang.

He told all this to Salvatore, the photographer, and Salvatore agreed that it was a very thorny problem, but Salvatore was thinking.

Mario was always going in to Materdei to see how Ciccio was

84

getting on and one evening Ciccio met him at the door as soon as he
got there. "It's all ready. Come and see." Mario walked down the
narrow passage which formed the entrance to the offices of the church
and followed Ciccio down the two broken stone steps to the place
which had been the church itself when the building had been used,
before the war.

The floor was of large flagstones and the only part of the church
left was a small stone altar. Over this rose a small dome, with a gallery.

It had been built at the time of the Baroque period of architecture
and the proportions were still beautiful, though now it was all cold
and grey.

Ciccio had had all this swept out and on the floor he had put the
eight palliasses, each one with a blanket; the helpers had asked their
families and friends if they could spare a blanket, and they had!

Mario's feelings were so deep at that moment he could not say anything. He thought of the Scugnizzi over the years trudging, as he
trudged, from street to street to find a sleeping place for the night.
And here waiting for them was shelter, with beds and food. He humbly
thanked God that he had given him this task to do.

Salvatore was working in his studio when the phone rang. "It's Mario," said the voice at the other end.

"Listen, I'd like you to come along again and, this time, bring your camera and a flash lamp. Take some photos. The boys will let you because they've taken to you, but the main thing is to take a photo which shows *me* quite clearly. Get my profile," he chuckled, "you know, they call me Crooked Nose for a nickname, well, get me in profile so that my crooked nose will show. Then, when I eventually tell them who I am, I can show them these photos. You see, when I've got them to Materdei I'll have to tell them I'm a priest and that I disguised myself as one of them in order to find out their needs."

"And when you tell them," broke in Salvatore, "you want to dress in your soutane, I suppose?"

"Oh, yes, of course, I must. It will be a very tricky business telling them. I'll have to time it just right!"

"I must say, you look quite different in your clerical clothes and in your Scugnizzi clothes. Even I can hardly recognise you when I come over to join the gang! All right, I'll take the photos tonight."

That evening he turned up with his camera and explained that he wanted to take some photos of the very "artistic" scene of them all crouched on the pavement. His heart sank when he said this, because nothing was further from his mind. Anyway, they let him take the photos and never asked to see them. Salvatore developed them and kept them safe for Mario.

* * *

Mario sat down with the other members of the gang and thought he had better make a point about it being so cold and miserable, and where were they going to find a place to sleep *that* night? They all felt pretty miserable—it was not too bad sleeping out in the summer, but now! It was still very cold and the only cosy place was on top of the gratings which were let into the pavement outside bakers' shops, where you could look down and see the baking of the bread. Warm air from the ovens always drifted up, indeed it was meant to, because the grating was for ventilating the bakehouse. But this method of sleeping out had its drawbacks—the smell of freshly-baked bread was too much of a penance to have to endure on an empty stomach!

"Well, you do look a miserable lot! And I don't blame you. It's

86

chilly *and* damp tonight." It was Salvatore. He shuddered with imaginary cold. "It gets into my bones. I don't know how you can stand it, night after night. Nino looks quite ill!"

The boys felt even colder than ever, and Nino coughed unhappily.

"What can we do about it?" asked Mario in his best Scugnizzo voice. "They all chase us away from doorsteps, and even bomb sites, if they see us."

"It's difficult." Salvatore seemed lost in thought; "I wish I could help you . . . just a minute . . ." then he seemed to be straining his mind to think of something as the boys all looked up at him.

"I know what it was! I heard the other day that somewhere, some priest has opened up a sort of hostel. People can go there and get a bed to sleep on and some food, and he charges *nothing at all*."

"Oh yes! I've heard of it too," said Mario.

"Have you! Well, why not try that. It can do no harm just trying it for a night."

"I don't believe it," said one of the boys, "A priest wouldn't do anything for nothing, just like that, he would want us to sweep out the church, or polish the candlesticks, or something."

"No, no! I heard say—I *wonder* where I heard it—that this was absolutely free."

"Well, where is it?" asked another boy.

Then Salvatore, who had talked this little play over with Mario the night before, said: "Oh, yes! I remember—it's at the Materdei church."

"Oh! That place up the road, all bombed out. I know it."

"I can just see them letting us in there—we can't just turn up and say we've come for the night, can we? They'll kick us out, say we haven't washed, or something!"

"Right! I know!" said Salvatore, "I'll go up there and tell them you're coming. I'll see the priest. You come up when you want to." And he went away.

The gang hung around, arguing.

Mario, exhausted, and so near the culmination of his efforts, felt he could not stand the strain one moment longer.

"Well! Shall we try this priest's place, then? We all know where Materdei is—let's go and find Salvatore there."

So off Mario went, very tired, ill and very hungry, walking through the streets as in a nightmare. He came to Materdei, and hung around like a real Scugnizzo looking for trouble. Some of the others drifted up. Mario rang the bell.

Pasquale and Vittorio opened the door. Mario the Scugnizzo, with the whole of his gang, walked in for their first night's rest and shelter.

CHAPTER 13

CLIMAX

"TAKE that! And that! And that!" On the steps of the San Carlo Theatre two young men were fighting, and one was definitely getting the better of the other. He was a vicious-looking character indeed. His torn clothes, unkempt hair, and expression as of a hunted animal, all showed him to be a Scugnizzo. But he was one of the older ones who formed quite separate gangs, and kept apart from the younger ones who were not yet hardened criminals.

The young man he was hitting seemed reluctant to fight back, although suffering from the terrible blows from the other's fists and kicks from his heavy boots. Soon he had been pushed back to the steps of the theatre where he sat down, breathing heavily, while the other went back to his gang, lounging comfortably on some straw round a charcoal fire.

After a time, the Scugnizzo on the steps got up and limped off while the gang followed him with their eyes. "Wonder who he is," said the one who had beaten him. "Well, anyway, I'll know him another time from that crooked nose of his!"

*   *   *

Mario was talking to Salvatore that evening. "You know, Salvatore, a professor who teaches at my school runs a paper. It's called *The Grain of Wheat*. I've talked to him about my months on the streets and how I have opened Materdei. He is writing an article about it all. Let's see your photos, you've taken so many since you first started." They both looked at the photos and chose some.

"When he puts that article in the paper, and some of your photos, I'll have the chance I've been waiting for to tell the boys that I'm a priest.

"All my gang already know of Materdei and they have told others about it. Pasquale too has gone about telling people the Scugnizzi can find a bed and shelter and food, and so has Ciccio, so, do you know, every night the place is *full* of Scugnizzi!"

89

"How wonderful, Mario!" said Salvatore.

Mario bowed his head. He felt that it was all wonderful too, and knew that because he had prayed and prayed, and asked Christ to guide him to know what next to do with his life, he had found the right thing at last, and all had gone as Christ had wanted it to. However, something nagged at the back of his mind; he was not sure whether he was to talk about it, but that something was a strange stop to all his plans and work.

"Salvatore!"

"Yes?"

"Well, last night I thought I would go to the San Carlo Theatre gang, sit down by their fire, say I was cold, and then tell them about Materdei . . . but . . ."

"Yes? What happened, Mario?"

"Well, the leader there kicked and punched me. I didn't want to fight back. I am a priest. So, I just don't know what to do now."

"That gang is the toughest of all and that boy—he's called Cicillo —is a really nasty character. Oh, Mario! Will you try again?"

"Yes, tomorrow," said Mario.

When Mario walked over to the San Carlo Theatre gang again he saw—could he believe his eyes?—Salvatore talking and chatting with them.

Of course, Salvatore, with his "Bohemian" appeal, was accepted by all the Scugnizzi, just as he had been that first night. And he wanted to help Mario. As Mario moved closer, he heard him talking to the boys:

"Have you heard of the Materdei, where a priest called Don Vesuvio gives food and shelter?"

"Yes, we have," the Scugnizzi said, "One of us went there one night and it was quite good."

Mario walked over and sat down.

"Oh!" said Salvatore, "Here's a lad who knows Don Vesuvio." And as they all looked at Mario, Salvatore took a photo. So he got his photo for *The Grain of Wheat*—Mario, dressed as a Scugnizzo, in the midst of the toughest gang of the lot. When Mario came with the paper and the article with the photo (it would be out on Saturday, he would dress as a priest, but with his broken nose which Cicillo had already noticed it would be easy for the boys to see it was the same person.

Salvatore took one or two more photos. Cicillo recognised Mario as the one he had fought against.

"So *you* know Don Vesuvio? Well, well, what does he look like?"

"What a difference!" Mario thought. "Last time I was here we were enemies. Now he's talking to me as friendly as can be. It's all due to Salvatore."

"Well," said Mario, "Would you like to meet Don Vesuvio?"

"Yes," said Cicillo, "When?"

Next Saturday, it was decided, Mario the Scugnizzo would bring Don Vesuvio to meet the gang.

Mario counted almost every hour till Saturday evening, and when, at last, it came he dressed in his soutane and his flat hat with meticulous care and walked to the San Carlo Theatre. The gang were there, talking to Salvatore who had with him a copy of *The Grain of Wheat*.

"Here's Don Vesuvio," said Salvatore. But the boys were too excited to notice. They were looking at the photos.

"Oh, look! There we all are. You, and you, and me . . ."

"Who's that?" said Salvatore, pointing to Mario's face among them in the photo, "He's not one of our gang!"

Cicillo had a look then—"Oh, that's easy! He's the one with the crooked nose I chucked out that night—and he came back again two or three nights ago and said he'd bring Don Vesuvio. Where is he?"

He looked up quickly and saw that Don Vesuvio, standing very still and calm and quietly among them, had exactly the same crooked nose as ... Mario the Scugnizzo.

"Are you ...?"

"I am Don Vesuvio and I am Mario of the crooked nose."

The Scugnizzi seemed to Mario to be all holding their breath. He did not know what would happen to him. They might be furious and attack him. They might believe or not.

All of a sudden they all, it seemed, were hugging him. Tears came into Father Mario's eyes. The Scugnizzi had understood in one split-second all that he had been trying to do in the past months and they were grateful. They, the rough, unkind, who stole, cheated, but who also had suffered great hardship and unkindness from humanity.

When he could manage to struggle free, Father Mario walked with them and Salvatore to Materdei where the same thing happened all over again with his own gang there.

That evening they all sang the old Neapolitan songs together and the dome echoed with them. Father Mario knew that he really had learnt just what the Scugnizzi needed, and that was Love, the Love that Christ taught His disciples to practise as the greatest of all the Commandments.

1974 POSTSCRIPT

MARIO BORRELLI is still at work in Naples. His hair is greyer now, but there is still plenty of it. He looks like a shaggy prophet. The work goes on.

But the work has changed because the needs of Naples have changed. Already, in the 1960s, he began to realise that it was not enough simply to deal with the boys. He had to deal with their families as well. The boys were coming to him from families who couldn't cope, and who thought they could get rid of their problems by handing them over to the *casa*. When the house is flooded, he thought, it is important to try and mop up, but it is even more important to find the tap and turn it off. He had to attack the *causes* of poverty and crime, not just the symptoms.

The causes, in the Naples of 1960, were there for all to see. Bits of spare ground were filled with "shanties". In 1962 Mario worked out that there were 24,410 people living in huts made of packing cases. The roofs were of corrugated iron, held in position by stones. There was hardboard in the gaps to serve as "windows". There were no lavatories, no proper water supply, no health services. There was no work for them to do either. The shanties bred hopelessness and crime.

Mario went to live in one of the shanty-towns in 1962. He had a little chapel made of packing cases. His candles were stuck in empty wine-bottles. But the shanty-dwellers never stayed anywhere very long. They were moved on, from place to place. The names of the shanty-towns make a sinister rosary: from Ponte Maddelena to Marinella; from Forte Vigliena to Scalesia. The names sound musical enough, but the reality was mud and disease. The sun doesn't always shine in Naples. Mario shared their life, just as he shared the lives of the *scugnizzi* earlier.

Mario's thinking began to change. The shanty-dwellers could improve their situation, but only if they worked together. They were not poor because they were lazy, but because they didn't know how to organise themselves. With the help of others, small improvements were made: they got rid of the rats, the children were inoculated against polio. "The first step in dealing with poverty", said Mario, "should be to say to the poor: 'You are more capable than you think you are, you *can* change your situation.'" That is what he told them, and they found it was true. It gave them hope.

Mario learned something else too. Even when housing was provided, it was often the wrong sort of housing. People were used to living on top of each other. So when they were moved into huge flats in the outskirts, they felt lonely and isolated. All the landmarks had gone. Their way of life had been destroyed. One old man complained he couldn't get his mule up to the fifth floor. The stupid animal refused to go into the lift. Mario learned that all the problems had links with other problems. Poverty had to be dealt with as a whole.

So he took some time off to study, and came to England to find out more about these questions. By the time he went back to Naples the shanties had been cleared away. That was progress. But much remained to be done. The *casa* continued. But in the 1970s it became a centre for all the people of Materdei, from the oldest to the youngest.

The children were bored at ordinary school. So he set up an afternoon school where they could talk in dialect, and paint, and do sculpture and make music. Some of the parents got interested, too, and started coming to classes. It is a cheerful, noisy place now. People can get medical help there: the best doctors offer their services for nothing. And there is free legal advice, too, for the people who are in trouble or who don't know how to fill in forms.

The Materdei area is being slowly changed. People are working together to improve things. Working together is something new for them. As Mario says: "There have been lots of tenors and sopranos from Naples, but who ever heard of a *choir* from Naples?" Among the poor of Naples, and thanks to the generosity of so many friends, the unheard of is happening.

PETER HEBBLETHWAITE

94